In the Kitchen
with
Your Favorite Chefs

Edited by Susan Pories, MD and Mary-Catherine Deibel

Drawings by Louis Kiley

For all the courageous women
who have battled breast cancer

and

In fond memory of Julia Child

To benefit the Hoffman Breast Center
at Mount Auburn Hospital

In the Kitchen
with
Your Favorite Chefs

Published by the Mount Auburn Hospital

website: www. mountauburnhospital.org

email: mahdevelopment@mah.org

IBSN 978-0-578-75826-8

"The world begins at a kitchen table.
No matter what, we must eat to live.

The gifts of earth are brought and prepared,
set on the table. So it has been since creation,
and it will go on."

-Joy Harjo
from: *Perhaps the World Ends Here*

Table of Contents

Permissions

"Tomato Broth and Artichoke Tortellini and Pistachio Avocado Pesto," "Oliver's Chicken Stew with Lemon, Tarragon, Parmesan Cheese, and Tiny Pasta," "Beets on a Plate with Goat Cheese, Fresh Figs, and Mint," and "Smoked Salmon Bundles with Arugula, Mascarpone Cheese, Chives, and Capers," copyright 1995 by Rialto/Jody Adams. Used by permission of Jody Adams.

"Curried Spaghetti with Roast Capon, Pinenuts and Raisins," "Beet Risotto with Arugula and Carpaccio of Beef," and "Polenta Pound Cake." Used by permission of Daniele Baliani.

"Lemon-Caper Sole," "Baltimore Style Crab Cake," "Chocolate Bread Pudding," "Clam Chowder," "Scrod Stuffed with Shrimp and Mushroom," and "Bluefish with Mustard Sauce." Used by permission of Roger Berkowitz and Richard Vellante, Legal Sea Foods.

"Pheasant and Fresh Waterchestnut Potstickers" and "Ginger-Glazed Shallots." Used by permission of Eric Brennan.

"Roast Rack of Lamb with Semolina and Spinach Gnocchi," "Risotto with Porcini," "Caciuccio-Tuscan Fish Stew," "Tuscan Grill's Linguine Giovanni," and "Vivo Restaurant Maine Lobster Fettuccine with Sweet Corn and Basil Butter." Used by permission of Jimmy Burke.

"Red Garlic Sauce: Rouille," "Simple Fish Stock," and "Hard Toasted French Bread Rounds: Croûtes" from *The Way to Cook: A Cookbook by Julia Child*, copyright © 1989 by Julia Child. Used by permission of Alfred A. Knopf, an imprint of the Knopf Doubleday Publishing Group, a division of Penguin Random House LLC. All rights reserved.

"Leapin' John." Used by permission of Kevin Conner.

"Yankee Pot Roast." Used by permission of Peter Davis.

"Foie Gras and Black Truffle Flan with Wild Mushroom Ragu and Mache," "Almond Crusted Snapper," and "Roasted Oysters." Used by permission of Todd English.

"Skillet Cooked Hanger Steak with Blue Cheese Butter," "Gratin of Mussels, Country Ham and Potatoes," "Braised Wild Mushrooms with Roasted Garlic Toasts," "Seared Sea Scallops with Green Onions and Tomatoes," "Chocolate Espresso Torte." Used by permission of Gordon Hamersley. "Souffléd Lemon Custard" from *Bistro Cooking at Home,* copyright © 2003 by Gordon Hamersley.

"Apple Charlotte with Apricot-Caramel Sauce," "Day Boat Lobster Salad with Orange Truffle Aioli and Fresh Harvest Beans," "Warmed Roquefort Flan with Duck Salad," "Deborah's Gazpacho with Pesto and Rock Shrimp," and "Roasted Sweet Red Pepper Soup," copyright 1992 by Deborah Hughes, UpStairs at the Pudding. Used by permission of Deborah Hughes and Mary-Catherine Deibel.

"Linguine with Lobster in Lemon Parsley sauce" and "Roasted Chicken Legs Mediterranean." Used by permission of Michela Larson.

"Chick Pea Panisses." Used by permission of Amanda Lydon.

"Ricotta and Goat Cheese Pillows with Slow Roasted Tomato Sauce and Black Olive Crumbs," and "Chestnut Bisque." Used by permission of Barbara Lynch.

"Pacific Northwest Dungeness Crab Ravioli with Thyme-Tomato Broth" and "Mistral Black Truffle Macaroni." Used by permission of Jamie Mammano.

"Brioche Stuffing" and "Chicken Boudin." Used by permission of Frank McClelland.

"Pan Roasted Atlantic Salmon with Fennel Saffron Tarragon with Extra Virgin Olive Oil Emulsion," "Salad of Grilled Pears and Endives with Cured Ham, Greens in Sage Oil and Lemon," "Chicken with Brined Vegetables (Giardiniera)," "Tunisian Tajine of Grilled Vegetables." Recipes by Moncef Meddeb used by permission of Alia Meddeb.

"Lamb Shank Tagine with Prunes and Apricots." Used by permission of Alia Meddeb.

"Boston Bouillabaisse (Straight Wharf Fish Soup)," "Cauliflower soup," "Sautéed Bay Scallops with Fall Puree of Squash and Apple," "Smoked Bluefish Pâté," "Broiled Salmon on a Bed of Warm Potatoes," "Pan-fried Scrod, Cod, or Haddock in an Egg Coating" from *The Victory Garden Fish and Vegetable Cookbook* by Marian Morash, copyright 1993. Used by permission of Marian Morash. "Sweet Potato-Chocolate Nut Cake" from the *Victory Garden Cookbook* by Marian Morash, copyright 1992. Used by permission of Sterling Lord Literistic, Inc.

"Curried Coconut Shrimp with Papaya-Saffron Relish," "Plaintain Crusted Red Snapper with Coconut Rice and Ahili Mohill served with Banana Chutney." Used by permission of Paul O'Connell.

"Swordfish Au Poivre with Parsnip Puree and Red Wine Braised Shallots," "Scallops Ceviche with Watermelon, Wild Mint, and Grapefruit." Used by permission of Ken Oringer.

"Country Apple Tart" from *Sweet Simplicity, Jacques Pépin's Fruit Desserts, Bay Books,* copyright 1999 Used by permission from Jacques Pépin. "Glossy Yellow Pepper Soup with Asparagus Garnish" from *Jacques Pépin's Kitchen: Encore with Claudine* , Bay Books. 1998. Used by permission from Jacques and Claudine Pépin.

"Marinated Salmon in Muscadet," "Mussel Soup," and "Lemon Mousse." Used by permission of Andrée Robert.

"Summer Striped Bass Salad," "Scallop and Nectarine Skewers with Grilled Red Pepper-Lime Sauce," "Simple Grilled Swordfish Skewers," "Peach and Chicken Skewers with Middle Eastern Shake and Simple Raisin Sauce," "Korean-Style Grilled Chicken Wings." Used by permission of Chris Schlesinger.

"Yukon Gold Potato Soup with Shrimp, Bacon, and Potatoes," "Asparagus Salad with Serrano Ham, Confit Tomato, Frisee and Red Onion," "Halibut with Wild Mushrooms and Truffle Vinaigrette." Used by permission of Michael Schlow.

"Spicy Baked Beans," "Pan Roasted Lobster with Whiskied Honey," "Maple Creme Brulee." Used by permission of Lydia Shire.

"Armenian Bean and Walnut Pâté," "Turkish Tarator Sauce," "Red Lentil and Carrot Kofte." Used by permission of Ana Sortun.

"Braised Atlantic Salmon with Leek, American Sturgeon Caviar and Creme Fraiche," "Caponata Le Bocage," "Warm Sweet Rice with Curried Fruits." Used by permission of Susanna Harwell-Tolini.

"Smoky Turkey Shu Mai in a Sweet Pea Broth" and "Blue Ginger Alaskan Butterfish with Soba Noodle Sushi." Used by permission of Ming Tsai.

"Parsnip Puree," "Cranberry-Black Walnut Pound Cake," and "Strawberry Shortcake" from *Jasper White's Cooking from New England* © 1989 Harper Collins, used by permission of Jasper White.

"Turnip Greens and Bottoms with Smoked Turkey," "Ms. Annie's Fried Shrimps," "Baked Turkey Wings with Vegetables and Country Gravy,"and "Triple S Chicken: Sweet, Spicy & Smokey Grilled Chicken." Used by permission of Michelle White.

"Insalata Supremo" and "MIDA Steak and Potatoes" used by permission of Douglass Williams.

Spot illustrations used by permission of Louis Kiley. All rights reserved.
Cover by Julianne Gilpin.
The text font is Granjon, which is the type face used in Julia Child's iconic book, *Mastering the Art of French Cooking* .

Preface

Dear Friends,

Julia Child was a great friend to Mount Auburn Hospital. She lived on Irving Street in Cambridge, walking distance from the hospital and took part in several fundraisers to benefit the hospital breast center. She herself was a breast cancer survivor and talked openly of her experience. Two of the most memorable events are commemorated here.

The first was in April 1998. As the Cambridge Chronicle reported at the time, culinary "grand dames" Julia Child and Marian Morash lent their cooking talents to a benefit held at the Royal Sonesta Boston that raised $72,000 for the Breast Center. At the time, this was the largest fundraiser ever held by the Mount Auburn Hospital Auxiliary. WGBH-TV's Russell Morash served as host while the two chefs prepared Boston Bouillabaisse. Many celebrated Boston chefs served on the honorary committee for the event. The other great event was held in October 2001 just before Julia Child left Cambridge to return to her native California. Radio talk show host Christopher Lydon served as Master of Ceremonies and toasts were made throughout the evening from many of the leaders in the culinary scene. TV's Arts & Entertainment Critic Joyce Kulhawik sang a culinary version of "You're the Top" to Julia (see Mignardise: A Musical Confection). The evening concluded with an auction of items from Julia's kitchen led by Russell Morash. When Gordon Hamersley, Chef-Owner of Hamersley's Bistro, offered a dinner for ten and another group of chefs offered a dinner for twelve, the bidding skyrocketed. At the end, this memorable benefit raised $80,000 for the Hoffman Breast Center at Mount Auburn Hospital.

For both of these events, the chefs donated recipes for a small cookbook, which was a keepsake for those who attended. Here, these many years later, we bring these recipes back for your culinary enjoyment and celebration. It has been a labor of love to connect with all of these fabulous chefs, and bring this unique collection of recipes to you. We are delighted to include several outstanding new contemporary chefs as well. Many of the chefs have shared special memories of their time with Julia Child. One favorite story comes from Michela Larson: *"I feel lucky to have lived in a time and place to have gotten to know her beyond her television personality. She was a terrific mentor—and terrifically generous with her time and talent. My older son still talks about the day we hosted her for lunch at our home for one of her many 80th birthday celebrations. He was our "server" and he helped set and decorate the table. We were just about finished but I felt that the table needed something more for such a momentous occasion. Christian promptly went upstairs to his room and returned with an armful of his most precious "super heroes." He said that she was a superhero and so the table should be finished with other superheroes in attendance. He was right—it looked terrific with Captain America, Superman, Spiderman, Wonder Woman, etc. striding down the center of the table. Julia loved it."*

I hope you enjoy these recipes as you step into the kitchen with your favorite chefs. And we thank you for your support of the Hoffman Breast Center. This support makes a difference for women with breast cancer, every day, ensuring the very best of care.

Sincerely,

Mary-Catherine Deibel and Susan E. Pories, MD

Julia Child: A Spectacular Lady

Julia McWilliams was born in Pasadena California in 1912. She attended Smith College in Massachusetts, following in her mother's footsteps. During World War II, she joined the Office of Strategic Services. She met her future husband Paul Cushing Child during the war. They were married in September 1946 and moved to Washington, D.C., where he had taken a position with the Foreign Service. When they were later stationed in Paris, France, in 1949, Julia enrolled at the famous Cordon Bleu cooking school and began her culinary career. She met Simone Beck and Louisette Bertholle there, and with them, started a cooking school called L'Ecole des Trois Gourmandes (School of the Three Gourmets). The three chefs began work on *Mastering the Art of French Cooking*, which was published in 1961 and was an immediate success. After Paul left the Foreign Service, they moved to Cambridge, Massachusetts. Julia Child went on to author or co-author many more successful cookbooks. She then began a weekly cooking show, *The French Chef*, in 1962, based on her books, which aired for a decade on WGBH television. Julia won many awards for her work, including a Peabody Award and an Emmy. She was a founder of the American Institute of Wine and Food and was the first woman elected to the Culinary Institute of America's Hall of Fame. She created the Julia Child Foundation for Gastronomy and Culinary Arts in 1995. Child won the Legion d'Honneur, France's highest honor and was awarded honorary doctorate degrees from numerous schools, including Harvard University and Brown University. Julia donated the kitchen from her Cambridge home to the Smithsonian Institution, where it has been restored as an exhibit at the National Museum of American History. Julia Child passed away in 2004 and left a legacy of celebrating the joy of cooking. The US Postal Service included Julia Child in the 2014 "Celebrity Chefs Forever" stamp series. For more information please see The website for the The Julia Child Foundation for Gastronomy and the Culinary Arts: https://juliachildfoundation.org
(photo credit: Julia Child in her kitchen as photographed by ©Lynn Gilbert, 1978, Cambridge, Mass. CC BY-SA 4.0)

Julia Child expresses her support for the Breast Center as Marian Morash looks on.

Roger Berkowitz of Legal Sea Foods presents Julia with a monkfish for the "Boston bouillabaisse."

About the Hoffman Breast Center

Photo Credit: Alyssa Peek

The Hoffman Breast Center is named for Alice Hoffman, the renowned novelist, whose generous support helped create an important resource that is designed to prioritize the health and wellness of women throughout our community. The mission of the center is to facilitate comprehensive patient-focused education, screening, diagnosis, and treatment of all aspects of breast health in a compassionate, professional, and supportive environment. The Hoffman Breast Center at Mount Auburn Hospital is accredited by the National Accreditation Program for Breast Centers (NAPBC), a national consortium of professional organizations dedicated to improving the quality of care for patients with breast cancer. We are very proud of this designation as it speaks to the excellent care we provide to our patients. When you are facing cancer, you want top-quality care delivered with compassion. It is our privilege to provide the very best cancer care at Mount Auburn Hospital, a Harvard Medical School-affiliated hospital, with a team of highly skilled providers who will take the time to listen to you and create treatment, support, and survivorship plans that fit your unique needs.

The Hoffman Breast Center
617-499-5755

NATIONAL ACCREDITATION PROGRAM FOR BREAST CENTERS
ACCREDITED BREAST CENTER

Appetizers

Smoked Bluefish Pâté
Chef Marian Morash

We originated this pâté years ago in Nantucket when fresh bluefish first began to be smoked in our local fish store. The pâté keeps beautifully for a few days and it is a most economical spread for a large party – you can double, triple, and more, this recipe. Makes 3 – 3 ½ cups.

Ingredients

½ lb smoked bluefish, skin on
1 lb cream cheese at room temperature
½ cup chopped red onion
¼ cup fresh lemon juice
1½ cups chopped parsley
Salt and freshly ground pepper

Alternative fish can be used. Smoked haddock, smoked salmon, smoked sable, almost any smoked fish will do, even smoked eel, but just adjust the amount of fish used depending on how "smoky" the fish tastes.

Preparation

Carefully remove the skin, bones, and the center line of dark flesh from the skin side of the bluefish and discard: you will have about ⅓ pound of smoked bluefish.

Flake the bluefish into small pieces. Put the cream cheese in a mixer bowl and beat to soften, then add the bluefish and mix well. Add the onion and lemon juice and beat all together. Taste and season with salt and pepper. Stir in the parsley and serve with Melba rounds, toasted thin rounds of French bread, or sourdough baguettes.

• Add a few tablespoons of yogurt or sour cream to lighten the mixture.

• Add horseradish, or mustard, or drops of hot pepper sauce to taste if you like.

Armenian Bean and Walnut Pâté
Chef Ana Sortun

Ingredients

1 cup soaked dark red kidney beans
2 cups water
¼ white onion, minced
1 bay leaf
4 Tbsp butter
½ tsp chopped garlic
¾ cup walnuts, lightly toasted
3 Tbsp mixed chopped dill, mint, and basil
¼ cup pomegranate seeds

Preparation

Bring beans to a boil with onion and bay leaf. Simmer until tender. Drain well and discard bay leaf. Puree with salt, pepper, walnuts, 1 tablespoon of the chopped herbs, butter, and chopped garlic.

Season well and spread onto a small baking sheet lined with saran wrap. Cool completely. Sprinkle generously with pomegranate and remaining fresh herbs, then roll into logs.

Chill again, before slicing.

Garnish with walnuts and dot with pomegranate molasses. Served as meze at Oleana with homemade string cheese and bread.

Ricotta and Goat Cheese Pillows with Slow Roasted Tomato Sauce and Black Olive Crumbs
Chef Barbara Lynch

Serves 8 as an appetizer.

Ingredients

10 plum tomatoes	4-5 cups all-purpose flour	½ cup goat cheese
1 onion, sliced thin	2 tsp salt	2 tsp flat-leaf parsley, chopped
4 cloves garlic, sliced thin	4 egg yolks	½ cup grated Parmesan cheese
1 cup olive oil	6 eggs, whole	Salt and pepper to taste
1 cup basil, sliced	½ cup ricotta	Semolina for sprinkling

Preparation

Preheat oven to 300 degrees. In a half hotel pan or large baking sheet, combine tomatoes, onions, garlic, oil, ½ cup basil, and salt and pepper. Cook uncovered for about 3-4 hours, or until tomatoes are slightly charred and soft. Allow to cool.

To make the pasta, sprinkle a pinch of flour on cutting board or work surface. Place 2 cups of flour and salt on the board and make a wide well in the middle. Crack the yolks and eggs into the well. With a fork, beat eggs along the perimeter of the well, bringing in small amount of flour and continuing all the way around until most of flour is absorbed. Knead the dough, turning it over and folding for about 3 minutes. The dough should have a slightly sticky touch, add remaining flour if it is too wet. Wrap the dough in plastic and allow it to rest for about ½ hour. In a small bowl, mix ricotta, goat cheese, parsley, Parmesan, and salt and pepper. Keep chilled until pasta has been rolled out. Roll out pasta gradually thinning the dough to $^1/_{16}$". Lay sheets flat, and cut it vertically in half. Place a teaspoon of filling at 2 inch intervals. Cover with the other layer of pasta and press down around the perimeter of each mound of ricotta to seal. Using a knife or pastry wheel, cut pasta in between ricotta mound, in a square shape. Separate each pillow and press lightly on the edges again to secure the seal or push out any excess air. Place on a sheet tray lightly sprinkled with semolina. To prepare, boil a pot of salted water and cook pillows 4 minutes or until they float. Top with some warm roasted tomatoes and remaining basil. Lay pillows on plate and garnish with black olive breadcrumbs (see below).

Black Olive Breadcrumbs

⅓ loaf day old bread, diced very small	½ cup olive oil to taste
3 Tbsp black olive paste	Salt and pepper

Preheat the oven to 375 degrees. Toss everything into a mixing bowl and place in a single layer on a sheet pan. Bake until crisp and browned, and stir once to evenly toast, about 5 minutes. Allow to cool until ready to use. Yield 2 cups.

Pheasant and Fresh Water Chestnut Potstickers with Ginger-Glazed Shallots
Chef Eric Brennan

Makes 16 potstickers or 4 appetizer portions

Ingredients for Potstickers

4 pheasant legs and thighs
1 cup kosher salt
1 cup brown sugar
2 Tbsp ground star anise
1 Tbsp fresh ground black pepper
16 round Goya skins (or wonton wrappers)
8 fresh water chestnuts (boiled, peeled and diced)

¼ cup minced chives
2 bay leaves
8 cloves garlic (crushed)
8 whole star anise
1 cinnamon stick
8 Shiitake mushrooms (sliced and sautéed)

Preparation for Potstickers

To cure pheasant, combine salt, brown sugar, ground anise, and pepper. Pack under and on top of pheasant legs. Cover and refrigerate for 6 hours. Rinse off cure and pat legs dry. Place pheasant in an oven-proof pot. Cover with cooking oil (or duck fat, if available). Add bay leaf, whole star anise, cinnamon, and garlic. Place parchment paper over top and cook in a 250-degree oven for approximately 4 hours or until meat is almost falling off the bone. Remove legs from oil, remove meat from bone and shred. Mix with chives, shiitake, water chestnuts, and a pinch of pepper. Place 1 tablespoon of mixture on the middle of each goya skin, egg wash the edges, and fold over into a half-moon. Crimp edges firmly. Lightly steam potstickers, or boil briefly, and add to a nonstick pan with a little of the fat in which the legs were cooked. Brown both sides and drain.

Ingredients for Ginger-Glazed Shallots

1 bulb ginger (sliced in quarters and smashed)
12 shallots, peeled
1 ½ oz Mirin (sweet rice wine)
1 cinnamon stick
4 star anise

1 squirt of fish sauce (Asian condiment)
2 thin chili peppers, minced
¼ cup of sugar

Preparation for Shallots

Combine all ingredients in a sauce pot, and simmer for 20 minutes (until shallots are soft). Remove star anise and cinnamon stick.

To Plate

Place 3 shallots and some of the shallot liquid in each bowl. Place some Thai basil, mint and cilantro in middle. Place 4 potstickers on top.

Smoky Turkey Shu Mai in a Sweet Pea Broth
Chef Ming Tsai

I'm a great lover of shu mai, those open-topped dumplings traditionally filled with a pork and shrimp mixture. For this East-West version, I use turkey and pureed chipotles in adobo-smoked jalapenos in a vinegar based sauce – for the filling. The chipotles, and not the turkey, provide the smoky flavor. These savory dumplings pair beautifully with the fresh, bright green broth in which they're served. Laced with a little chile oil, the shu mai make a sensational starter or light lunch. Serves 4.

Beverage Tip
Chilled Gamay (Cru Beaujolais) from Brouilly, Moulin-A-Vent)

Ingredients

Broth
2 Tbsp canola oil
2 cups roughly chopped yellow onions
2 cloves garlic crushed
2 cups chicken stock or low-sodium canned broth
Salt and freshly ground white pepper
2 cups fresh English peas or frozen peas
1 cup spinach leaves, well washed, tough stems removed
4 Tbsp butter (½ stick)

Filling
1 lb ground turkey
1 Tbsp pureed chipotles in adobo (see tip)
1 egg
¼ cup heavy cream
4 Tbsp butter (½ stick), roughly chopped and frozen
4 scallions, green parts only, sliced ⅛ inch thick
Salt & freshly ground pepper
12 square wonton wrappers
4 tsp chile oil for garnish

Preparation

To make broth, heat a medium saucepan over medium heat. Add the oil and swirl to coat the bottom of the pan. When the oil shimmers, add the onions and garlic, reduce the heat to medium-low, cover, and cook until the vegetables are soft and their moisture is released, about 8 minutes. Add the stock and season to taste with the salt and pepper. The broth should be salty.

Increase the heat to high and bring to a boil. Add the peas and spinach and cook until soft, 6 to 8 minutes, adding the spinach for the last 2 minutes. With a hand or standard blender, puree the mixture. Add the butter and puree until very smooth. Correct the seasonings. Keep warm over very low heat.

To make the filling, in a food processor, combine the turkey, pureed chipotle, egg, and cream, and puree. Add the butter all at once and pulse just to blend. Transfer the mixture to a chilled bowl and fold in the scallions. Season with the salt and pepper to taste.

To form the shu mai, hold 1 wonton wrapper in your hand. Place ½ tbsp. of the filling in the center of the wrapper. Bring the sides of the wrapper up around the filling, pleating the wrapper as you go. Tap the dumpling against the work surface to flatten it. Repeat with the remaining wrappers and filling.

Set up a steamer. Line the steamer baskets with lettuce leaves or spray with vegetable spray to prevent sticking. Add the shu mai, and steam until they soften and fat gathers near their openings, about 8 minutes.

Divide the shu mai among 4 soup plates. Add the broth, drizzle with the chile oil, and serve.

MING'S TIPS

Make sure to cook the peas in stock that is sufficiently salty; this is what maintains the bright color of the peas.

Puree a small can of the chipotles in adobo beforehand and store it in a tightly sealed container for up to 3 months. Leftovers make a fiery accompaniment to burgers, ribs, or chicken.

Smoked Salmon Bundles with Arugula, Mascarpone Cheese, Chives, and Capers
Chef Jody Adams

Serves 6 as hors d'oeuvres.

Advance Planning

The rolls may be done a day ahead, minus the arugula, and kept refrigerated. Before serving, push three arugula leaves into the top end of each roll.

Ingredients

4 oz mascarpone cheese
1 Tbsp capers
1 Tbsp minced chives
1 tsp lemon juice
Salt and freshly ground pepper
48 small tender arugula leaves
12 oz smoked salmon – 12 large thin slices

Preparation

Mix the mascarpone cheese with the capers, the chives, and lemon juice. Season with salt and pepper.

Lay the salmon slices out flat on a cutting board so that they're all arranged horizontally in front of you with plenty of spaces about and below each slice. If necessary, fill and roll the slices in batches.

Put a spoonful of the mascarpone mixture on the narrow end of each slice.

Arrange six arugula leaves on a slice of salmon, the bases of the leaves all scrunched up together atop the mascarpone. The idea is to arrange the leaves so that once the salmon is rolled up three leaves will project several inches from each end of the salmon roll. Now, starting at the narrow end, roll the salmon up like a jelly roll.

Cut the roll in half, crosswise. Stand the halves upright, the ends of the arugula leaves pointing upward, in a shallow glass dish large enough to hold all 24 half-rolls in the refrigerator until you're ready to serve them. Repeat the process for the remaining slices. Refrigerate the halves until serving.

To Serve

Place four upright half-rolls on each appetizer plate and serve.

Soups, Salads, and Side Dishes

Clam Chowder from Legal Sea Foods
Chefs Roger Berkowitz and Richard Vellante

Serves 8.

Ingredients

4 quarts littleneck clams (about 1⅔ cup cooked and chopped)
1 clove garlic, chopped
1 cup water
2 ounces salt pork, finely chopped
2 cups chopped onions
3 Tbsp flour
1 ½ lb potatoes, peeled, and diced into ½ inch cubes
4 ½ cups clam broth
3 cups fish stock
2 cups light cream
Oyster crackers (optional)

Preparation

Clean the clams and place them in a large pot along with the garlic and water. Steam the clams just until opened, about 6 to 10 minutes, depending upon their size. Drain and shell the clams, reserving the broth. Mince the clam flesh, and set aside. Filter the clam broth either through coffee filters or cheesecloth and set aside.

In a large, heavy pot slowly render the salt pork. Remove the cracklings and set them aside. Slowly cook the onions in the fat for about 6 minutes, stirring frequently, or until cooked through but not browned. Stir in the flour and cook, stirring, for 3 minutes. Add the reserved clam broth and fish stock, and whisk to remove any flour lumps. Bring the liquid to a boil, add the potatoes, lower the heat, and simmer until the potatoes are cooked through, about 15 minutes.

Stir in the reserved clams, salt-pork cracklings, and light cream. Heat the chowder until it is the temperature you prefer. Serve in large soup bowls with oyster crackers on the side.

Roasted Sweet Red Pepper Soup
Chef Deborah Hughes and Mary-Catherine Deibel

Serves approximately 6 to 8 people.

Ingredients

20 extra large red peppers
½ lb butter
2 Anaheim peppers
2 Scotch bonnet peppers ½ cup balsamic vinegar

6 sprigs rosemary
1 qt best quality heavy cream
4 large white kitchen onions
1 head of garlic, chopped
Kosher salt to taste

Preparation

Roast 20 extra large red peppers over an open flame. Do not let skins turn ashen and gray. After roasting, immediately blanch and peel blistered peppers. Roasted peppers are not enhanced by sitting in water. Drain and coarsely chop peppers.

Melt ¼ lb. butter in one very large or two large heavy bottomed sauté pans. Add ½ cup balsamic vinegar, 2 coarsely chopped Anaheim peppers, 2 coarsely chopped Scotch Bonnet peppers, and 2 rosemary sprigs. Simmer briefly, then add chopped peppers. Cook for about two hours over very low heat. This process naturally caramelizes the peppers and melts the flavors together.

In a heavy-bottomed pot, reduce by half 1 qt heavy cream. Remove from heat.

When peppers have softened considerably (about two hours) remove from heat. Cool slightly. Divide peppers into several batches and lightly puree in a blender, using the on/off switch. Do not overly homogenize.

Place in large enamel-coated cast iron soup pot and add cream. Cook slowly to combine flavors – approximately 20 minutes. Do not cover or allow to boil.

In a separate pot, combine 4 chopped onions, ¼ lb butter, 4 large rosemary sprigs, and 1 chopped head of garlic. Cook over low heat until wilted and softened, approximately 30 minutes. Puree when cooked and add to soup pot. Season to taste.

Deborah's Gazpacho with Pesto and Rock Shrimp
Chef Deborah Hughes and Mary-Catherine Deibel

This gazpacho can be made several days ahead of time and is served room temperature rather than chilled, as in the conventional variety of gazpacho.

Ingredients

Seed 4 dozen plum tomatoes. Leave skin on and dice.
6 bunches fresh basil.
Peel and very finely chop 6+ cloves of garlic.
1 Tbsp salt
¾ cup balsamic vinegar
½ cup good quality extra virgin olive oil.

Preparation

Mix garlic with basil in a blender.
Add salt, vinegar, and oil.
Combine the basil-garlic pesto with the plum tomatoes, and leave at room temperature for several hours.

Quantities of vegetables can then be added. Your choice should depend on the quality of the ingredients and personal taste.

All should be as finely diced as possible:
4 English cucumbers, scored with a fork and seeded; leave skin on
6 green peppers
6 red peppers
6 yellow peppers
4 bunches of scallions
2 purple onions
2 bunches of fresh chives

Other options to add just before serving:
Whole yellow Sweetheart Napa Valley tomatoes
Sliced avocado
Grilled chicken
Grilled sweet corn, scraped off the cob
Grilled sliced eggplant
Fresh little rock shrimp, marinated in lemon juice and good olive oil (especially recommended)
Dollop of basil walnut or other pesto

Cauliflower Soup
Chef Marian Morash

A hearty cauliflower soup I tasted in Denmark almost 35 years ago convinced me of the suitability of this pale ivory vegetable for soup courses. Serves 6-8.

Ingredients

1 ¾ lb trimmed cauliflower
2-3 Tbsp fresh lemon juice
Salt
2 Tbsp butter
1 cup chopped leeks
½ cup chopped celery
5-6 cups chicken broth
½ cup light cream (optional)
Pepper, freshly ground
2-3 Tbsp chopped chives

Preparation

Separate the cauliflower florets from the stems, and cut any thick skin off the stems. Take ¾ pound of the cauliflower florets and cut them into ½ pieces, keeping their flower shape as much as possible. Chop the remaining cauliflower and set aside in a separate bowl.

Bring a large pot of water to a boil, add 2 tablespoons of lemon juice, and ½ teaspoon salt, and drop florets into the water. (The chopped pieces will be used later.) Blanch the florets for 2-3 minute or until they are just tender. Drain them immediately, run under cold water to stop the cooking action, or drop them into a bowl of ice water, drain again, and reserve to one side.

Heat the butter in the same pot, add the leeks and celery, and cook, stirring, until they have wilted and picked up flavor for 3-4 minutes. Add the chopped raw cauliflower and 5 cups of broth, bring to a boil, reduce the heat, cover, and simmer until tender, about 10-15 minutes, or until the cauliflower is tender. Puree the soup in a food processor or blender, leaving the mixture slightly rough. Add more broth if necessary, and add the cream if you like.

Season with salt and pepper, and more lemon juice if desired. Add the reserved cooked cauliflower florets, stir gently, reheat, and serve topped with chives.

Day Boat Lobster Salad with
Orange Truffle Aioli and Fresh Harvest Beans
Chef Deborah Hughes and Mary-Catherine Deibel

Serves 6 to 8.

Ingredients

6 -1½ lb soft shell cull lobsters
Juice of one lemon
Juice of one lime

For Mayonnaise

1 cup homemade mayonnaise, or
good quality commercial mayonnaise
Orange oil
1 Tbsp truffle oil
2 Tbsp fresh orange juice
Finely chopped orange zest

For Chive Oil

1 cup canola oil
1 large clove garlic
1 cup blanched fresh chives, chopped finely
2 cups haricots verts
1 cup fresh corn
1 cup fresh peas
1 cup fresh fava or cranberry beans
Segments of 2 oranges, trimmed of all
white membrane
One head frisse lettuce

Preparation

Add truffle oil, a good squeeze of fresh orange juice, finely chopped orange zest, and several drops of orange oil to mayonnaise.

Cook lobster in boiling water for 10 minutes. Chill, then clean, discarding shells and reserving all lobster meat. Cut into ¾ inch to 1 inch pieces. Salt, and add lemon and lime juice.

Fold the lobster into the mayonnaise and chill. Add blanched finely chopped cup of fresh chives and finely chopped garlic to canola oil, and pulse in food processor. Salt to taste.

Blanch beans quickly, and shock in cold water to retain color. Blanch corn and peas.

To Serve

Place haricots verts criss-cross around the perimeters of a dinner plate. Place frisse in top center of plate and cover with lobster salad. Drizzle with chive oil.
Strew a handful of fava or cranberry beans and a small amount of corn kernels and peas randomly on the plate. Arrange orange segments around perimeter of plate. Decorate with flower petals.

Chestnut Bisque
Chef Barbara Lynch

Serves 6 as an appetizer.

Ingredients

For Soup
½ lb bacon sliced or cut into ½ inch dice
1 onion
2 stalks celery, cut into ½ inch dice
1 celery root, peeled cut into ½ inch dice (about 8 ounces)
1 Idaho potato, peeled, cut into ½ inch dice
3 cups chestnuts, frozen and peeled
2 cups ruby port wine
6 cups chicken stock
2 cups heavy cream to taste
Salt & pepper

For Garnish
1 cup dry white cooking wine
1 carrot peeled, cut into 1 inch chunks
2 stalks celery, cut into 1 inch chunks
1 onion
2 dried bay leaves
5 black peppercorns, whole
½ lb veal sweetbreads, fresh
2 Tbsp grapeseed or canola oil
¼ cup chestnuts, previously frozen, thawed and sliced
1 lb chanterelles or hedgehog mushrooms, fresh and cleaned to taste
Salt & pepper

Preparation

Heat a medium saucepot, and add the bacon. Cook on low to medium heat, stirring occasionally, until the bacon has slightly browned and has started to render its fat. Add the onion and cook slowly until soft and translucent. Add the celery and stir, cooking until soft. Add the celery root, potato, and chestnuts. Stir to incorporate. Deglaze with the port wine, and simmer on low heat until it is almost reduced completely. Add the chicken stock and continue to cook until the chestnuts have completely softened. Finish with heavy cream and bring the soup up to a full boil. Remove from the heat. Using a hand held blender puree the soup until smooth. Strain the soup through a fine sieve and adjust the seasonings with salt and pepper.

Poach the sweetbreads by making a court bouillon. In a saucepot, combine the white wine, carrots, onions, celery, bay leaves, and peppercorns with ½ gallon of water. Bring the bouillon up to a simmer and add the sweetbreads. Cook on medium heat about 12 minutes until the sweetbreads are firm and they are no longer pink. Remove them from the bouillon and plunge them into ice water to stop the cooking. You may discard the bouillon. Once the sweetbreads have cooled, place them into a container, and cover them with plastic wrap. Place a large object of considerable weight, with a flat bottom surface, directly on top of the sweetbreads and press the sweetbreads for a minimum of one hour.

Clean the sweetbreads by removing them from their press. Pull the outer membrane off from the surface of each sweetbread lobe and separate the sweetbreads into small nuggets removing any additional membrane you find.

To serve the soup, heat a sauté pan and add in the oil. Heat until just before the oil smokes, and add the nuggets of sweetbread. Sauté them until they are crispy and brown. Add in the sliced chestnuts and mushrooms. Sauté until lightly browned and soft. Season with salt and pepper.

It makes a beautiful presentation to split the hot garnish into 6 individual bowls and pour the soup at the table in front of the guests. Alternately, the soup may simply be ladled into the bowls on top of the garnish.

Tomato Broth and Artichoke Tortelli
with Pistachio Avocado Pesto
Chef Jody Adams

Serves 4.

Ingredients

Artichoke Filling
Extra virgin olive oil, about 3 cups
1 small onion, thinly sliced
3 cloves garlic, smashed
2 large artichokes
1 lemon zested (zest saved) and cut in half
1 bay leaf
1 sprig thyme
Salt and freshly ground black pepper
12 - 3 inch square fresh pasta sheets
1 egg cracked and beaten with 2 tsp water to form an egg wash
Semolina flour for dusting

Avocado-Pistachio Pesto
Yield about 1 cup
1 cup packed basil leaves, washed and dried well
⅓ cup extra virgin olive oil
1 clove garlic, finely minced
3 Tbsp pistachio nuts
2 Tbsp grated Parmesan cheese
Kosher salt and freshly ground pepper to taste
2 Tbsp diced avocado
1 small block Parmesan cheese

Broth
2 Tbsp extra virgin olive oil
1 small onion, cut into ¼ inch dice
½ stalk celery, cut into ¼ inch dice
½ head fennel, cut into ¼ inch dice
2 cloves garlic, smashed
2 lb ripe tomatoes
2 basil stems
Salt and freshly ground black pepper
1-2 tbsp sugar to taste

Preparation

Artichokes

To make the artichokes, trim the leaves off the artichokes until you get to the yellow leaves. Rub with lemon. Trim the tough outer layer of the stem and bottom. Rub with lemon. Cut in half and rub with lemon. Heat 1 cup olive oil in a heavy bottom sauce pan over medium heat. Add onion and garlic and cook until tender, about 10 minutes, season with salt and pepper. Add artichokes, lemon zest, and herbs, and cover completely with additional olive oil. Season with salt and simmer until artichoke bottoms are tender, about 30 minutes. Drain the artichokes, onions, and garlic, and save the olive oil for another use. Remove the leaves and choke from the artichoke. Puree the artichoke bottoms, with the onions and garlic, in a food processor. Strain if the puree is too fibrous. The puree should be quite thick. Season with salt and pepper and lemon juice, if necessary.

To make the tortelli, lay out 4 pasta sheets. Brush the sheets with egg wash. Put a spoonful of the artichoke mixture in the center of the pasta sheets. Starting with a corner, roll the pasta, enclosing the filling. The pasta forms the shape of a wrapped candy. Set on a cookie sheet sprinkled with semolina flour. Cover and refrigerate any leftover filling.

Pesto

Put basil leaves in the bowl of a food processor, with the motor running. Add oil in a steady stream and process until the herbs are finely chopped, about 1 minute. Add garlic and pistachios and process another 20 seconds. The pistachios should be finely chopped, but not a paste. Transfer to a small bowl with the Parmesan cheese. Stir well. Add the diced avocado and season again with salt and pepper. Toss gently. Cover and refrigerate.

Broth

Heat olive oil in a large sauté pan. Add the onions, celery, fennel, and garlic, season with salt and pepper, and cook until tender, about 10 minutes. Cut tomatoes into quarters. Puree with a hand-held emersion mixer or a food processor. Strain into the sauce pan with the other vegetables. Simmer 30 minutes. Strain and keep warm. Bring a large pot of water to a boil. Add salt. When the water returns to a boil, add the tortelli and cook until pasta is tender, 1 to 2 minutes.

To Serve

Place 3 tortelli in each of 4 warm shallow soup bowls. Pour the broth over the pasta, top with a spoonful of pesto and grate Parmesan cheese over the top.
Serve immediately.

Glossy Yellow Pepper Soup
with Asparagus Garnish
Chefs Jacques and Claudine Pépin

This elegant soup is the perfect opener for a formal dinner. Essentially a puree
of yellow peppers garnished with spears of asparagus, the soup's gloss and
creamy texture are achieved by emulsifying the mixture with a hand blender before
it is served. Serves 4.

Ingredients

8 oz asparagus, preferably large stalks with tight heads, for garnish
2½ cups water
3 yellow peppers (1⅓ lb), cut into 1-inch pieces
1 large potato (9 oz), peeled and cut into 1-inch pieces
1 large onion (8 oz) peeled and cut into 1-inch pieces
3 cloves garlic, peeled
1 tsp salt
1 ½ tsp sugar
¼ tsp freshly ground black pepper
2 Tbsp unsalted butter
2 Tbsp extra virgin olive oil

Preparation

Peel the lower third of the asparagus stalks, and discard the trimmings. Cut the
asparagus on the bias into slices, ¼ - to – ½ inch thick. (You should have about
1½ cups.) Bring ½ cup of the water to a boil in a saucepan, and add the asparagus
pieces. Bring the water back to a boil, and boil the asparagus for 30 seconds. Drain,
reserving the cooking juices, and set the cooked asparagus pieces aside
in a bowl.

Place the yellow peppers, potatoes, onion, garlic, salt, sugar, and pepper in a large
saucepan, and add the remaining 2 cups of water. Bring to a boil, add the reserved
asparagus cooking juices, cover, and reduce the heat to medium. Cook the mixture
for 30 minutes, then push it through a food mill fitted with a fine screen to remove
the skin of the yellow peppers. Yield: 6 cups.

Add the butter and oil, and emulsify the mixture with an electric hand blender until
it is smooth and creamy appearance. Add the reserved asparagus, stir, heat through,
and serve.

Insalata Supremo
Chef Douglass Williams

Serves 4.

Ingredients

Dressing

¼ cup red wine vinegar
½ cup olive oil
1 tsp sugar
2 tsp Dijon mustard
Pinch each of salt and pepper

Salad Base

1 lb tender greens (such as gem lettuces, really anything you find yummy, tender and refreshing).
¼ lb thin shaved radishes on a mandolin (watermelon, breakfast or even turnip from the farmers market)
¼ cup picked mint leaves, torn
¼ cup fresh dill, picked and torn
Your choice of your favorite stone fruit such as plum, peach, nectarine, cherries, or orange citrus (cut or segmented to no bigger than an inch)
¼ cup Pecorino Romano

Preparation

For the dressing, put all contents into a bottle or plastic container and shake hard for 10 seconds. This can be made ahead of time and lasts for a week in the fridge.
For the salad, combine lettuce, pinch of salt, pinch of pepper, radishes, mint, and dill. Dress the salad lightly. Then add cheese and fruit, mix once more.
Taste, adjust dressing amount, and serve.

Salad of Grilled Pears and Endives with Cured Ham, Greens in Sage Oil, and Lemon
Chef Moncef Meddeb

Ingredients

Two ripe pears (Anjou, Comice, Bartlett, or Asian) peeled, cored and quartered
24 endive leaves (about 4 endives) washed, patted dry
4 oz mesclun greens, washed, spun dry
4 Tbsp extra virgin olive oil
1 Tbsp lemon juice
Salt
Coarse cracked black pepper

Sage Oil

1 bunch minced fresh sage
½ cup extra virgin olive oil

Preparation

Put minced sage into blender. Blend at high speed while drizzling the olive oil in a steady stream. Blend thoroughly, then set aside.
Preheat grill (if grill is not available, set a medium non-stick sauté pan on high heat).
Lightly brush pears and endives with some of the sage oil.
Grill pears until grill marks are set. Set aside.
Very briefly (5 to 10 seconds) grill endive leaves, concave side facing the grill. Set aside.

Serving

Toss mesclun in center of 4 plates. Set 6 endive leaves on either side of the mesclun.

Place 2 grilled pear quarters on either side of the greens. Dab pears with a little bit of coarse black pepper.

Interweave prosciutto in between endive leaves.

Drizzle endive, pears, and ham with sage oil and lemon juice.

Optional

Garnish with sage leaves deep fried for 30 seconds.

Mussel Soup
Chef Andrée Robert

Ingredients

Fish stock
Tomatoes, peeled, seeded, and chopped
Onion, finely diced
Garlic, finely diced
Parsley, finely chopped
Bay leaf
Mussels (washed)
White wine
Olive oil

Preparation

Cook the mussels in half of the white wine and fish stock. When the shells are open take off the fire and cool. Separate the mussels from the stock and remove the meat from the shells. (Discard the shells)

Sauté the onion in olive oil gently until translucent. Add the garlic. Add chopped tomatoes, fish stock, liquid from the mussels, bay leaf, and season to taste. When ready to serve, add the parsley and mussels at the last minute.

Mistral Black Truffle Macaroni
Chef Jamie Mammano

Serves 4.

Ingredients

12 oz fresh ditalini pasta (or substitute dried)
1½ cups heavy cream
8 oz Madeira sauce (Madeira flavored demi-glace)
½ cup grated Reggiano-Parmesan cheese
1 medium size Perigord black truffle (shaved very thin)
4 Tbsp whole butter

Preparation

Bring Madeira sauce to boil, whisk in half of shaved truffles. Reserve warm.

Boil fresh pasta in salted water approximately three to four minutes until just done and strain.

While pasta is cooking, quickly heat heavy cream to a boil, and reduce slightly, whisk in remaining butter and Parmesan cheese, and finish by tossing in cooked pasta.

Presentation

Spoon warm Madeira truffle sauce onto hot soup plate and carefully place hot pasta on top. Top with remaining sliced truffles and serve immediately.

Yukon Gold Potato Soup with Shrimp, Bacon, and Potatoes
Chef Michael Schlow

Makes 4 quarts of soup.

Ingredients

3-4 Yukon gold potatoes (peeled and cut into medium size pieces)
1 white onion (peeled and med dice)
1 celery root (peeled med dice)
1 leek (white part only) sliced
1 quart vegetable stock
3 quarts milk
1 cup créme fraiche
2 Tbsp butter
Salt and white pepper

Garnish

Diced shrimp (cooked)
Smoked bacon (diced and cooked)
Potatoes (diced and blanched)
Finely sliced chives

Preparation

Place all ingredients (with the exception of the crème fraiche and butter) in a large soup pot. Gently cook over medium heat until potatoes are tender. Remove from heat and puree in a high speed blender until smooth. Season with salt and pepper, add crème fraiche and butter, and readjust seasoning. Adjust consistency with vegetable stock.

Garnish bowls with shrimp, bacon, and potatoes, and then pour hot soup over the top. Garnish with sliced chives.

Asparagus Salad with Serrano Ham, Confit Tomato, Frisee, and Red Onion
Chef Michael Schlow

Makes 4 salad courses.

Ingredients

16 asparagus spears, blanched
12 thin slices Serrano ham
4 large Tbsp tomato confit (chopped)
2 Tbsp chopped shallot
1 tsp chopped fresh thyme
6 oz extra virgin olive oil
3 oz sherry vinegar
1 red onion
4 bunches frisee
3 tsp sliced chives
Salt and black pepper

Preparation

Place three slices of Serrano ham on 4 dinner plates.
Marinate the asparagus with a pinch of shallot, a pinch of thyme, salt, pepper, olive oil, and some of the sherry vinegar. Place 4 asparagus spears on top of the ham. Combine the tomato with some of the shallot, some thyme, olive oil, salt and pepper. Make a quenelle of the tomato and place at two o'clock on the plate. Dress the frisee with olive oil, sherry vinegar, chives, thyme, salt, pepper, and the sliced onions. Place the frisee on top of the asparagus. Drizzle the plate with olive oil and serve.

Fruits and Vegetables

Spicy Baked Beans
Chef Lydia Shire

Serves 6.

Ingredients

1 cup dried kidney beans
½ cup dried cannellini beans
½ cup dried Great Northern or navy beans
2 sprigs fresh thyme
1 Tbsp cumin seeds
1 Tbsp olive oil
1 large onion, chopped
1 carrot, chopped
½ lb smoked slab bacon, in ½-by-1-inch nuggets
1 jalapeno pepper, seeded and chopped
2 cloves garlic, chopped

½ cup crushed canned tomatoes
4 ripe plum tomatoes, diced
¼ cup maple syrup
¼ light brown sugar
1 bay leaf
Grated rind of 1 orange
½ Tbsp crushed black peppercorns
½ cup chopped fresh coriander leaves
¼ cup cider vinegar, or more, to taste
Salt to taste

Preparation

Place all beans in a bowl, cover with water to a depth of 2 inches, add thyme, and soak at least 4 hours.

Heat a heavy 3-quart casserole. Add cumin seeds, and cook, stirring until they dance around and smell toasty. Remove them.

Add the oil, onion, carrot, and bacon to casserole, and sauté over medium heat about 10 minutes, until the bacon is golden. Stir in the jalapeno, garlic, and toasted cumin seeds.

Preheat oven to 250 degrees.

Drain beans, and add them along with canned and fresh tomatoes, maple syrup, brown sugar, bay leaf, orange rind, and crushed peppercorns. Stir in all but 1 tablespoon of the coriander, and add 3 cups of water. Cover and bring to a slow simmer. Place in the oven and cook 2 hours.

Add vinegar and salt to taste. Return to oven two and half hours longer, until the liquid has been absorbed but the beans are still moist. Add seasonings, adding more vinegar and salt if needed. Sprinkle with remaining coriander and serve.

Warm Sweet Rice with Curried Fruits
Chefs Edward and Susanna Tolini

Ingredients

1 cup uncooked long-grain rice
2 cup milk
Pinch of salt
½ cup peeled and cubed pineapple
½ cup peeled, cored, and cubed apple
½ cup peeled and cubed banana
½ cup cored and cubed pear
3 Tbsp unsalted butter
2 Tbsp curry powder, to taste
1 ½ cup heavy cream

Preparation

Put rice, milk and salt in sauce pan, cover, bring to boil, stir with a fork. Reduce heat very low, cover tightly, cook until rice is tender and milk absorbed, about 18 minutes. Prepare fruits. Melt butter in wide saucepan over low heat. Stir in curry powder to make a paste, cooking a minute until curry's fragrance is released. Toss fruit with curry mixture to coat on all sides. Add cream and bring to a boil. Remove from heat and cover.

To serve, make a ring of rice or a mound onto each individual serving plate.

Spoon the curried fruit over the rice. Garnish it with the fresh berries and a spring of mint.

Risotto with Porcini
Chef Jimmy Burke

Ingredients

3 Tbsp olive oil
1 cup minced onion
12 oz fresh porcini sliced
2 cup rice
7 cup hot chicken stock
Salt and pepper
2 Tbsp butter
½ cup Parmesan cheese

Preparation

In a medium sauce pot heat oil and sauté onion until golden. Add
mushrooms and sauté chicken until tender. Add the rice and stir to coat.
Add some hot chicken stock and stir constantly until it is absorbed.
Continue adding stock in small batches (enough to moisten rice) and cook
until absorbed. Continue stirring until mixture is creamy, and al dente.
Remove from heat and stir in butter and cheese. Season and serve.

Moroccan-Style Vegetable Stew
Chefs Ihsan and Valerie Gurdal

From Formaggio's Kitchen comes a hearty, flavorful vegetable stew. Serve as a main dish over couscous or a side dish accompanied by roast leg of lamb. Serves 6-8.

Ingredients

1 lb Spanish onions
1 head garlic, minced
6 lb chopped mixed vegetables of your choice: carrots, zucchini, okra, squash, sweet potatoes, green beans
1-28 oz can plum tomatoes, coarsely chopped with liquid
2-16 oz cans chickpeas
4 Tbsp cumin
1 Tbsp sweet paprika
1 tsp coriander, ground
1 tsp cinnamon
Salt and pepper to taste

Preparation

Sauté onions in 4 Tbsp olive oil until golden brown.
Add garlic and sauté until fragrant.
Add spices, mix well, then add the chopped vegetables and tomatoes.
Cook, covered, about one hour until meltingly tender.
Add chick-peas, heat through.
Serve over couscous or rice.

Braised Wild Mushrooms with Roasted Garlic Toasts
Chef Gordon Hamersley

Ingredients

1 lb wild mushrooms
3 shallots - minced
2 cloves garlic - minced
1 pinch herbs (thyme, marjoram)
6 Tbsp roasted garlic powder
Salt and pepper
White wine
1 thumbnail sweet butter
Olive oil
6-8 croutons - toasted
Watercress for garnish

Preparation

Clean the mushrooms with a soft brush or kitchen towel. Heat some olive oil in a sauté pan and add the mushrooms. Sear for two to three minutes until they are beginning to lose their juices. Add the wine, garlic, herbs, salt and pepper, and stew until the mushrooms are cooked and the juices are concentrated and flavorful. Add a thumbnail of butter to the pan to make the sauce rich and velvety.

Meanwhile, toast the croutons by sprinkling them with salt and pepper and olive oil, and baking them in the oven for about eight minutes. Spread with garlic purée during the last three minutes of the cooking.

To serve

Place one of the croutons on each plate and top with the braised mushrooms. Garnish with a few sprigs of watercress.

Tunisian Tajine of Grilled Vegetables
Chef Moncef Meddeb

Ingredients

12 oz red and green bell peppers
8 oz fresh plum tomato
6 oz Anaheim chilis
2 medium onions
3½ oz Gruyere or Swiss Cheese
1 oz Parmesan
3 ½ oz stale bread
1 Tbsp olive oil
6 phyllo leaves
2 oz cooked potato (diced)
1 oz capers
Grated rind of two lemons
⅔ oz butter
¼ cup melted butter
8 whole eggs
1 Tbsp tomato paste

Preparation

Grill or char the peppers, chilies, tomatoes, and onion. Peel, seed and dice the charred vegetables, mix in the coriander, and season to taste.

Grate the stale bread and Parmesan. Dice the Gruyere. Break eggs into a bowl. Beat lightly.

Set a sauté pan on medium heat, add 1 Tbsp olive oil and tomato paste, add vegetable mix and potato. Stir.

Add bread crumbs and cheese, combine eggs and vegetable mix. Add ⅔ oz butter. Mix well.

Line Genoese Pan with phyllo brushed with melted butter. Pour mixture. Wrap and seal.

Bake 30 minutes or until done. Cool down a few minutes. Unmold. Cut into wedges and serve.

Tuscan Grill's Linguine Giovanni
Chef Jimmy Burke

Serves 4 as first course or 2-3 as entrée.

Ingredients

1 lb imported linguine
1 Tbsp chopped garlic
1 cup extra virgin olive oil
1 tsp crushed red pepper (optional)
½ bunch basil leaves cut lengthwise
½ bunch chopped fresh flat leaf parsley
½ bunch chopped chives
2 each large beefsteak tomatoes, seeded, and rough cut.
½ cup freshly grated Parmesan cheese
Salt and pepper to taste

Preparation

Lightly sauté garlic and crushed red pepper in olive oil, do not brown,
turn off heat, and let stand.

Bring a 6-quart pot of lightly salted water to boil, place the linguine in the
boiling water, and stir well to prevent pasta from sticking together.

While the pasta is cooking, reheat the olive oil, add the fresh tomatoes,
and warm slightly.

When the pasta is cooked, strain, and toss with the oil tomato mixture in
a bowl or sauté pan.

Add the fresh herbs and Parmesan cheese, season with salt and black
pepper, and serve immediately.

Beets on a Plate with Goat Cheese, Fresh Figs, and Mint
Chef Jody Adams

Serves 4.

Ingredients

1 lb beets
¼ of an orange, including skin (optional)
Salt and freshly ground black pepper
4 tsp freshly squeezed orange juice
½ lb arugula
1 shallot, peeled and thinly sliced
4 Tbsp extra virgin olive oil
2 Tbsp balsamic vinegar
4 oz soft goat cheese
6 figs, cut in half
1 Tbsp mint leaves, cut into very fine strips

Preparation

Preheat oven to 400 degrees.

Put the beets in a small saucepan, cover with water, add orange, 2 teaspoons salt, ¼ teaspoon pepper. Bring to a boil, reduce the heat and simmer until tender, 30-40 minutes. Cool.

To peel the beets, put them in a tea towel and rub to remove the skin. Slice the beets into ¼ inch thick rounds using a mandolin or a sharp knife. Arrange the beets in concentric circles on 4 plates, forming a six inch disc. Season the beets with salt and pepper and a teaspoon of orange juice.

Toss the arugula and the sliced shallots with the olive oil and vinegar and season with ½ teaspoon salt and ¼ teaspoon pepper. Set a mound of arugula in the center of each plate. Put a spoonful of goat cheese on the arugula and garnish with three fig halves. Sprinkle with the mint.

Red Lentil and Carrot Kofte
Chef Ana Sortun

Makes about 6 patties.

Ingredients

¼ cup extra virgin olive oil
1 cup diced carrots
¼ cup finely chopped red bell pepper
½ tsp dried red chile flakes, preferably Maras or Aleppo pepper
1 cup chopped leeks or onion
½ tsp ground turmeric
1 tsp dried oregano
2 tsp ground cumin
1 cup red lentils
1 Tbsp tomato paste
1 cup fine bulgur
optional one egg

Optional toppings—
buttered buns
roasted poblano peppers, sliced and roasted delicate squash rings, lettuce leaves,

Preparation

In a medium sized sauce pot, sauté the carrots, pepper, spices, and leeks in olive oil with 1 tablespoon water and 1 tablespoon olive oil until very tender, about 8 minutes. Rinse the red lentils and immediately stir them into the vegetables. They will become sticky if you let them sit too long after they are rinsed. Stir in the tomato paste and another tablespoon of olive oil. Add 2 teaspoons of salt and 3 cups of water, and simmer until the lentils and vegetables are very soft and falling apart, and the lentils are thick but still soupy.

Stir in the fine bulgur and let it absorb. This part is very important as it helps the patties stay together when they are pan fried.

Place the dough in the bowl of a KitchenAid mixer and knead it until it is smooth and creamy, about 5 minutes using the paddle attachment. Add the remaining olive oil and the egg and mix for another minute until everything is broken down and it's creamy and the consistency of cookie dough. Re-season with salt, and red chiles, and form into 6-8 patties. Pan fry them in olive oil and butter on each side for until golden brown, about 4 minutes each side.

Caponata Le Bocage
Chefs Edward and Susanna Tolini

Caponata is a favorite dish of Ed and Susanna Tolini. For a full meal they suggest serving the piquant vegetable salad on a bed of radicchio topped with silvers of Parmesan or Romano cheese, along with good crusty bread and red wine. About 6 servings.

Ingredients

1 large eggplant
1 lb mushrooms, quartered
1 small head cauliflower, cut into florets
½ cup red or white wine vinegar
About 1 cup olive oil
2 large cloves garlic, chopped
2 Tbsp chopped fresh parsley
1 tsp crushed fresh rosemary
1 tsp fresh thyme

1 tsp crushed fresh oregano
¾ cup tomato puree
½ cup black Greek olives in brine
½ cup green olives
8 oz can of artichoke hearts
4 oz can of pepperoncini
3 oz jar of cocktail onions
Salt and pepper

Preparation

Peel the eggplant and cut it into large dice. Sprinkle generously with salt and allow it to bleed for several hours overnight. Rinse the eggplant under cold water, drain thoroughly, and pat dry with towels.

Blanch the mushrooms and cauliflower separately in salted water and drain well. While still warm, put them in a large bowl and sprinkle with vinegar. Stir occasionally as they cool.

Cover bottom of large skillet with ¼ inch of olive oil. Over medium heat sauté eggplant in batches, adding oil as needed. As eggplant colors, add it to mushrooms and cauliflower. Put remaining oil in another pan and soften garlic without letting it brown. Stir in herbs and tomato puree, bring to boil, and immediately pour over vegetables. Stir in black and green olives, artichoke hearts, pepperoncini and onions. Season to taste with salt and pepper – be careful because the olives' saltiness will become more prominent as the mixture marinates.

Let the caponata marinate at least 24 hours, covered and chilled (it will keep several weeks). The basic recipe can be varied according to taste; for instance, you can eliminate the olives and add capers. Bring it to room temperature before serving.

Chick Pea Panisses
Chef Amanda Lydon

Ingredients

8 cloves garlic
1 quart whole milk
7 oz chickpea flour
1 cup canned chick peas
2 Tbsp toasted whole cumin seed
2 Tbsp toasted whole coriander
1 tsp red pepper flakes
1 Tbsp whole fennel seed
2 Tbsp butter
1 Tbsp kosher salt
½ Tbsp coarsely ground pepper
Chopped parsley

Preparation

Heat the olive oil in a deep-sided sauté pan. Sweat the onion and garlic until translucent. Add the milk and bring to a boil. Whisk in the chickpea flour in a steady stream and cook stirring frequently until the polenta has thickened. Continue to cook, stirring constantly, until the polenta has dried out, about 8-10 minutes. Add the chopped chickpeas, spices, butter, and seasoning. Check the seasoning and adjust if necessary. Transfer the polenta to a half sheet pan lined with parchment paper. Smooth the surface of the polenta into an even rectangle and chill until firm, at least 4 hours, preferably overnight. Cut polenta into desired shape, and fry at 350 degrees or until deep golden.

Harissa Mayonnaise
6 egg yolks at room temperature
2 Tbsp Dijon mustard
Salt, white pepper
2 Tbsp lemon juice or red wine vinegar
3 cup neutral flavored oil
⅓ cup harissa
¼ cup chopped parsley

Combine the yolks with the mustard, lemon, salt, and pepper. Whisk in the oil, a little at a time, until incorporated, add the harissa incrementally to taste. Add the chopped parsley directly before serving. Garnish the chickpea fries with spicy mayonnaise, Lucques olives, and purslane salad dressed with lemon, extra virgin olive oil, mustard, salt, and pepper.

Parsnip Purée
Chef Jasper White

The parsnip has always been very popular in New England. Until I moved to Boston, I had never eaten parsnips; now I consider them one of the most underrated of all vegetables. The parsnip has a unique sweet herbaceous flavor, especially the spring dug. I am often asked what spices I use in the parsnip purée at my restaurant, and people seem surprised when I answer "None-just parsnips and butter." Serves 4-6 as a side dish.

Ingredients

2 lb parsnips
½ cup milk
8 Tbsp unsalted butter
Salt

Preparation

Peel the parsnips and cut off the very top. Bring a large pot of salted water to boil. Add the parsnips and cook until they are well done (about 10 to 15 minutes). Put in a colander and allow to drain. While the parsnips are draining, heat the milk in a small pot.

Combine the parsnips and hot milk in a food processor or blender. Puree and add the butter a little at a time until all is worked in. Season with salt (very little will be needed) and serve hot. The puree can be cooled off and reheated later if desired.

Turnip Greens and Bottoms with Smoked Turkey
Chef Michelle White

I love this recipe because you can use so many different kinds of leafy greens, from collards to mustards, to Swiss chard and kale. I have even made this recipe using baby beet greens, so delicious. Mix them up and have fun. Serves 5-7.

Ingredients

2 bunches turnip greens
1 large or two small turnip bottoms
1 smoked turkey wing-cut up in 6 pieces (or can omit)
20 oz chicken or vegetable broth
Season to taste, can add crushed pepper flakes and garlic cloves

Preparation

Wash and wipe each leaf then cut into half inch strips. Place in bowl.
Wash and peel turnip bottoms, then cut each into six pieces. Chunky pieces, not too small.

In a large pot with tight lid, add chicken broth to the pot with smoked meat. Boil for 30 minutes. Don't allow moisture to boil out and add water as needed to keep the smoked turkey bones covered.

Cook until the smoked turkey is tender then add greens and cook until tender. Add turnip bottoms last. Cook until tender 10 to 15 minutes.

Seafood

Boston "Bouillabaisse"
Chefs Julia Child and Marian Morash

A Mediterranean bouillabaisse is a thing of beauty, a dramatic production of selected local fish served whole on a platter with the fragrant soup served separately in a tureen. This version simplifies the preparation but preserves the basic concept of fresh local seafood richly flavored with the fragrance of olive oil, garlic, tomatoes, and onions. Served with a red garlic sauce – the classic rouille – and toasted rounds of French bread if you like, and it's hard to imagine a more delicious fish dish. This is a great company dish because so much can be prepared ahead. The fish stock can be made weeks ahead and frozen.

The soup base and the rouille can be made the day before serving and refrigerated. All that's left to do is cut some French bread, if desired, and add impeccably fresh fish to the reheated soup base. And, as we say in Boston, "Bon Appetit." (Serves 6-8.)

Ingredients

3-4 Tbsp fruity olive oil
3-4 cups thinly sliced onions or combination onions and leeks
6 cups peeled, seeded and roughly chopped ripe tomatoes*
Herb bouquet, wrapped in washed cheesecloth:
    4 sprigs parsley, 4 cloves peeled garlic, 1 tsp fresh thyme, 1 bay leaf,
    ¼ tsp fennel seed, 3 to 4 strips dried orange peel or ½ tsp bottled dried peel
2 quarts fish stock (recipe follows)
Salt and freshly ground pepper
Hot pepper sauce
2 ½-3 lb skinned and boned 2-inch chunks cod, haddock, monkfish, striped bass,
    cusk, or other firm-fleshed white fish
2-3 pinches saffron threads
Pernod (optional)
Chopped parsley
Rouille (recipe follows)
French bread rounds, recipe follows (optional)

Preparation

In a non-aluminum-lined 8-quart soup pot, heat the oil, add the onions, and cook, stirring occasionally, over medium high heat until they are wilted and golden, about 10 minutes. Stir in the tomatoes, bringing the mixture to a boil, cover, reduce the heat, and cook gently for 5 minutes to release the juice of the tomatoes. Uncover the pan and boil gently for 4-5 minutes to reduce the liquid.

Add the herb bouquet and the fish stock. Bring the mixture to a boil, reduce the heat, and simmer for 30 minutes. Season with salt and freshly ground pepper and a few drops of hot pepper sauce. Remove and discard the herb bouquet. (Cool and refrigerate the soup base at this point, if you like.)

Just before serving, bring the soup base to a boil. Drop in the chunks of fish and the saffron threads. Bring the soup to a gentle boil again and cook until the fish turns opaque, about 4-5 minutes. Add a splash of Pernod, if desired. Serve in warm soup bowls, sprinkle with chopped parsley, and serve rouille on the side to stir into the soup. Pass toasted French bread rounds, if you like.

Alternatively, place 2 toasted French bread rounds in each warmed wide soup plate, top with a spoonful of the rouille, and ladle on the fish, then soup, and finish with a sprinkling of parsley.

* Use garden-ripened tomatoes or a combination of fresh tomatoes and canned drained and seeded plum tomatoes.

You can substitute shellfish such as sea scallops or chunks of lobster for some of the fish.

Fish Stock
Chefs Julia Child and Marian Morash

This recipe makes about 6 quarts of fish stock. Use what you need and freeze the extra – it's a kitchen treasure.

Ingredients

10 lb fresh fish frames, such as haddock, cod, halibut, bass
3-4 stalks celery, roughly chopped
1 onion, roughly chopped
2 sprigs of fresh thyme
½ bottle dry vermouth or dry white wine

Preparation

Cut out and discard the gills of the fish frames. Remove and discard any skin, viscera or blood, and wash the frames very well. Chop the frames into large pieces.

Place all the ingredients in a large stock pot and add enough water to cover by at least 1 inch. Bring to a boil, skim off any foam, reduce heat and simmer for 20 minutes. Carefully strain the stock through a fine strainer, cool and chill immediately.

Once the fish stock is strained, you may boil the stock for 15 minutes to reduce and strengthen the flavor, if you wish.

Red Garlic Sauce: Rouille
Chefs Julia Child and Marian Morash

This marvelous sauce for all garlic lovers makes any fine fish soup even more splendid. To eliminate concern over using raw eggs in an uncooked recipe, substitute liquid pasteurized eggs. (Makes 1 ½ cups, serves 6-8.)

Ingredients

6 large cloves of garlic, peeled
¼ tsp salt
18 or so large leaves of fresh basil, or 1 ½ tsp dried savory, oregano or thyme
¾ cup lightly pressed down crumbs from homemade type fresh white bread
2-3 Tbsp hot soup (or milk)
3 egg yolks
⅓ cup canned red pimentos, drained
¾ to 1 cup fruity olive oil
Drops of hot pepper sauce
Salt and freshly ground pepper

Special Equipment Suggested
A mortar and pestle, or heavy bowl and pounding instrument of some sort, a garlic press and hand-held electric beater are useful. It is essential here that the garlic be pureed into a fine paste — the food processor or blender chops rather than purees. Although you could use the processor rather than mixer at the point where you add the egg yolks and oil, it hardly seems worthwhile for a small quantity of sauce.

Preparation

Puree the garlic in a heavy bowl, add the salt, and pound into a paste. Continue pounding while adding the herbs; when well mashed and blended, pound in the bread crumbs and soup base or milk. When they have formed a paste, pound in the egg yolks. At this point switch to the electric beater or a whisk, and beat a minute or more, until thicker and sticky. Finally, start beating in the oil by small driblets, as though making a mayonnaise. This should be a thick heavy sauce. Season to taste with pepper sauce, and salt and pepper.

—May be made a day in advance; cover and refrigerate. Let come to room temperature before stirring up, to avoid possible curdling.

Hand-Toasted French Bread Rounds: Croutes
Chefs Julia Child and Marian Morash

For 18 rounds.

Ingredients

1 loaf of French bread 16 inches long — the homemade type with body
½ cup or so olive oil, optional
1 cup grated Parmesan, hard Jack, or Swiss cheese, optional

Preparation

Slice the bread into rounds ¾ inch think, arrange in one layer on a baking sheet or sheets, and dry out for 25-30 minutes in a preheated 325 degree oven, until a light brown and crisp through. If you wish, spread the toasted rounds with a ¼ inch layer of grated cheese, drizzle on a few drops of oil, and brown lightly under the broiler.

— May be done in advance and kept in a warming oven for an hour, or wrap and freeze them.

Broiled Salmon on a Bed of Warm Potatoes
Chef Marian Morash

The salmon can be prepared for broiling well ahead and refrigerated. The potato "stew" can be made slightly in advance and reheated while the salmon broils just before serving. Serves 4.

Ingredients

1½-lb salmon fillet
Vegetable oil
1½-lb peeled and sliced potatoes
1½ cups salmon stock, fish stock, or unsalted chicken broth
½ cup dry vermouth or white wine
6 Tbsp butter
½ lb sliced mushrooms
½ cup sliced scallions (thin sliced on the diagonal)
Salt and freshly ground pepper
1 Tbsp chopped fresh dill

Preparation

Skin the salmon and remove any bones. Slice the fillet diagonally into ½-inch strips. Brush the strips with oil and lay them on a nonstick baking sheet. Cover and refrigerate until ready to cook. Put the potatoes, stock, vermouth or white wine, and 4 tablespoons of the butter into a 4-quart saucepan and bring to a boil. Reduce the heat, partially cover, and simmer until the potatoes are just tender. Lift the potatoes with a slotted spoon to a flat dish or pan; measure 1 generous cup of potato and return it to the saucepan, then spread the remainder out in the flat dish. Pour the liquid and potato from the sauce pan into a food processor or blender and puree the mixture. Return the puree to the saucepan and cook gently to reduce to about 2 cups of liquid.

Melt the remaining 2 tablespoons of butter in a sauté pan, add the mushrooms and scallions, and cook over medium heat until the vegetables are wilted and lightly colored. Add this mixture and the reserve potatoes to the pureed liquid and heat slowly. Season with salt and freshly ground pepper.

Place the tray of salmon strips under a preheated broiler 4 inches from the heat. Broil for 2 minutes or until just cooked through.

Divide the potato stew among 4 warm shallow soup plates or dishes with enough depth to accommodate the sauce. Place the salmon strips on top of the stew, sprinkle with the dill, and serve. Add other vegetables, such as blanched snow peas or finely chopped and sautéed red peppers.

Braised Atlantic Salmon with Leeks, American Sturgeon Caviar, and Crème Fraiche
Chefs Edward and Susanna Tolini

4 portions.

Ingredients

24 oz. salmon fillet (skinless)
2 each leek stalks
3 Tbsp butter (unsalted)
1 Tbsp olive oil
6 oz white wine
4 Tbsp American Sturgeon Caviar
4 tsp of American Golden Caviar
¼ cup crème fraiche
Salt and pepper
Tin foil strips (to shape the salmon)
Butcher's twine

Preparation

To prepare the salmon fillet – remove the pin bones. Cut the fillet into eight equal pieces.

To prepare the leeks – trim off the dark green portion and root end. Cut the remaining stalk lengthwise, then into thin half-moon shapes. Wash thoroughly, making sure to dislodge any sand. Braise the leeks in 2 tablespoons butter, covered until wilted, about 5 to 10 minutes. Do not brown.

Cut four strips of aluminum foil 2 inches x 12 inches each. Fold in half lengthwise. Butter each strip of aluminum, place the two portions of salmon back to back and wrap with a strip of aluminum and secure with butcher's twine.

Stuff each portion of salmon with some of the braised leeks.

Heat a sauté pan with the oil, sear the salmon on the bottom side 2 to 3 minutes. Remove the excess oil, add the wine, salt and pepper to taste, cover and place in the 350-degree oven for 10 to 12 minutes. Remove the fish from the pan and keep warm. Place the pan on the stove under high heat and reduce the white wine by half. Add the crème fraiche, bring to a boil and add the American Sturgeon Caviar.

Serve immediately. Place the fish on dinner plate, remove the foil and butcher's twine, and serve the sauce over each portion. To garnish each portion, place a teaspoon of American Golden Caviar on the top of each.

Pan Roasted Atlantic Salmon with Fennel, Saffron, and Tarragon, with Extra Virgin Olive Oil Emulsion
Chef Moncef Meddeb

Ingredients
4 - 7 oz salmon fillets skin on

Rub
2 Tbsp minced fennel fronds
1 Tbsp finely grated lemon rind
2 Tbsp extra virgin olive oil

Emulsion
6 medium fennel bulbs or 4 large, trimmed and quartered
1 pinch Spanish saffron
2 Tbsp extra virgin olive oil
1 Tbsp minced fresh tarragon
2 tsp fresh lemon juice, salt, pepper
1 Tbsp coarse sea salt
1 Tbsp cracked black pepper
4 sprigs fresh tarragon

Preparation

Rub
Mix all ingredients and spread over the flesh side of salmon fillets

Emulsion
Juice fennel into saucepan. Place over high heat, bring to a boil. Simmer until reduced by ¾. Strain. Add saffron and minced tarragon. Simmer 2 to 3 minutes. Transfer to blender. Add a pinch of salt and black pepper, and lemon juice. Blend in high speed for one minute. Transfer to a cup or through a funnel into a plastic squeeze bottle. Keep at room temperature.

Cooking the Salmon
Heat a 12 or 10 inch non-stick skillet, on medium/high heat. Sprinkle coarse sea salt and black pepper on salmon fillets. Place fillets skin side down in skillet, reduce heat, cover, cook 4-5 minutes until top of fish is slightly translucent and skin side is nicely crisp.

To Serve
Warm 4 plates. Drizzle a little emulsion in center of each plate. Cut each fillet in half on the bias. Place 2 halves on each plate; 1 half crisp side up, one half flesh side up. Drizzle more emulsion in zigzag patterns. Garnish with a sprig of tarragon.

Sautéed Bay Scallops with Fall Puree of Squash and Apple
Chef Marian Morash

Family scalloping season in Massachusetts begins in October, a month before the commercial season does. We put on chest-high waders and carry nets to scoop up the delicate sweet shellfish. This simple sauté – no flour, no bread crumbs, no batter – is all the scallops need, and they are gone so quickly we are soon back in our waders looking for our nets again. The seasonal squash-and-apple puree accentuates the sweetness of the scallops; it can be made well ahead, allowing one to devote the day to scalloping. (Recipe for squash-and-apple puree follows).

Serves 4.

Ingredients

1½ lb scallops
4-6 Tbsp butter
Salt and freshly ground pepper
Lemon wedges

Preparation

To prepare the scallops: Remove any tough cartilage on the sides of the scallops, wipe off any bits of shell, and pat dry. In a sauté pan large enough to hold the scallops in one layer without crowding (or use two sauté pans or cook in two batches) heat 4 tablespoons of butter. When the butter bubbles, add the scallops and cook for 2-2½ minutes, turning and tossing them after one minute of cooking. The scallops should just turn opaque. Remove the scallops to a warm serving platter, season with salt and freshly ground pepper, and serve with lemon wedges and the squash-and-apple puree.

- Use small sea scallops

- Use fresh sweet virgin olive oil in place of butter to sauté the scallops

- Cook 2 tablespoons of finely chopped shallots in the butter until wilted before adding the scallops. Cook the scallops and shallots, remove the scallops to a warm platter, deglaze the pan with 2-3 tablespoons dry vermouth or white wine, and pour the deglazing sauce over the scallops.

Squash-and-Apple Puree
Chef Marian Morash

Makes about 4 cups.

Ingredients

3 lb winter squash (Waltham butternut squash, buttercup etc.)
2 apples
Salt and freshly ground pepper
1-2 Tbsp finely grated orange peel (optional)
Pinch ginger or cinnamon

Preparation

Peel and halve the squash, remove the seeds and cut the flesh into 1-2 inch cubes.
Peel, core and quarter the apples. Bring 1-inch of water in a steamer to a boil. Place
the squash and the apples in the steamer basket, cover, and steam until the squash is
soft, about 15-20 minutes. Remove to a bowl and mash together to the consistency
you prefer. Season with salt and freshly ground pepper, and add the grated orange
peel and ginger or cinnamon, if desired. Keep warm if serving shortly, or cool,
cover and refrigerate, and reheat just before serving.

Variations for Squash

Add 2 tbsp of butter to the squash when you puree it

Add the butter to the squash puree, spread into a buttered 1 ½ qt baking dish dot
with additional butter if desired, and reheat in a preheated 350 degree oven for 30
minutes.

Russell Morash's Favorite Recipe: Pan-Fried Scrod, Cod, or Haddock in an Egg Coating
Chef Marian Morash

My husband says this is his favorite fish recipe, and if he ever has to request a last meal, this is it. The usual way of coating fish to be fried in batter is to dip the fish in beaten eggs, then dredge it in flour. This recipe reverses the order. The egg wash on the outside of the floured fish produces a soft "skin," which makes the fish seem all the more tender. Serve with "Squash-and-Apple Puree" (see recipe). Alternative fish: almost any firm-fleshed fish fillets. Serves 4.

Ingredients

1½ - 2 lb skinned scrod, cod, or haddock fillets
½ cup of flour
Salt and freshly ground pepper
3-4 Tbsp light olive oil
2 eggs beaten with 1 tsp water
Lemon wedges

Preparation

Remove any bones from the fish and cut the fillets into 4 equal portions. Place the flour in a flat dish or pie pan and season it with salt and freshly ground pepper.

In a sauté pan large enough to hold the fish in one layer, or in two pans, heat the oil. Dredge the fish in the flour, shaking off any excess, then dip it in the beaten egg, letting any excess coating drip off. Place the fish in the pan and cook slowly over medium heat for 3-4 minutes, or until the bottom coating is golden. Turn the fish and cook 3-4 minutes longer, depending on the thickness of the fish. Thinner tail ends will be done first. Remove to warm serving platter and serve immediately with lemon wedges.

Blue Ginger Alaskan Butterfish
with Soba Noodle Sushi
Chef Ming Tsai

I consider this my signature dish – it's been on the menu at Blue Ginger since day one, and people can't seem to get enough of it. It's evolved along the way and it's definitely a keeper. You might say it is a synthesis of two great dishes I ate and admired: the miso-brushed yakitoris I enjoyed in Osaka, and miso black cod, a great dish created by Nobu Matsuhisa. My dish is a real flavor-texture revelation – unusual and truly satisfying. I'm going on about this dish, but it truly kicks bass! Serves 4.

Beverage Tip: Toasted Oak, Vanilla Chardonnay (Mirimar Torres, any Le Montrachet)

Ingredients

1 cup light miso (shiro-miso)
½ cup Mirin (sweet Japanese rice wine)
½ cup sake
1 tbsp finely chopped ginger
½ cup canola oil
¼ cup sugar
4 - 5x3 inch pieces skinless butterfish cut from the fillet about 7 ounces apart

Sushi

½ lb dried soba noodles
¼ cup chopped fresh cilantro
¼ cup chopped scallions, green parts only
2 tbsp soy sauce
1 tbsp finely chopped ginger
2 tbsp rice wine vinegar
2 tbsp wasabi oil
4 tbsp chopped pickled ginger or gari
Salt and freshly ground black pepper
4 sheets toasted nori
1 cucumber, peeled, seeded, and julienned
2 red bell pepper, cored, seeded, and julienned
1 yellow bell pepper, cored, seeded, and julienned
10 ounces wakame salad
Freshly ground black pepper
Soy syrup
¼ cup toasted sesame seeds

Preparation

In a medium non-reactive bowl, combine the miso, mirin, sake, ginger, oil and sugar, and stir to blend. Add the butterfish, turn to coat, and marinate, covered and refrigerated, overnight.

To make the sushi, bring a large quantity of salted water to a boil. Fill a medium bowl with water and add ice. Add the noodles to the boiling water and cook until slightly softer than al dente, about 8 minutes. Drain and transfer noodles to ice water. When cold drain well. In a large bowl combine the noodles, cilantro, scallions, soy sauce, chopped ginger, vinegar, wasabi oil, and 2 tablespoons of the pickled ginger and toss to blend. Season with salt and pepper to taste.

Have a small bowl of water handy. Place a sheet of nori shiny side down on the rolling mat with a long edge toward you. Evenly spread a ¼ inch layer of the noodle mixture on the bottom half of the nori and top the upper third of the mixture with 3 to 4 strips of the cucumber and 2 pieces of each of the peppers. Roll and gently but firmly press the mat to seal. Allow the roll to rest, seam side down for 2 minutes. Repeat with remaining nori and filling ingredients. Cover the rolls lightly with plastic wrap and set aside.

Prepare an outdoor grill or preheat the broiler. Wipe the marinade from the fish and season it with pepper to taste. Grill or broil the fish, turning it once until just cooked through, 10 to 12 minutes. Meanwhile, cut each roll into 5 pieces, 3 straight across and 2 diagonally.

Divide the sushi pieces among 4 plates. Add a small mound of the salad, if using, to each with a piece of the fish. Drizzle over the soy syrup and wasabi oil, garnish with the sesame seeds and remaining pickled ginger and serve.

Wasabi Oil

This delightfully pungent oil is a wonderful way to enjoy wasabi flavor without what I call "wasabi blast." It's delicious drizzled on grilled fish or added to mayonnaise (in the proportion of 1 part oil to 4 parts mayo) for sandwiches. The oil will keep in an airtight container, refrigerated, for about two weeks, though it loses its zip over time. For extra pungency, reduce the quantity of canola oil to ⅓ cup oil.

Makes about 1 cup:
½ cup wasabi powder
2 tbsp Mirin (Japanese sweet sake)
2 tsp sugar
½ cup canola oil

In a small stainless-steel bowl, combine the wasabi powder, mirin and sugar and whisk to blend. Add a little less than ½ cup of water gradually, whisking until a pancake batter-like puree is formed. Whisk in the oil. Let stand for 10 minutes before using.

Soy Syrup

This thickish flavoring is a perfect seasoning or garnish for fish and all types of sushi. Store it tightly covered, in the fridge, where it will last for a month. (In a pinch, you can substitute kechap manis, the Indonesian sweet soy sauce, for soy syrup.)

Makes about 2 cups:

  2 cups soy sauce
  ½ cup brown sugar
  Juice of 1 lime

In a medium saucepan, combine the soy sauce, brown sugar, and lime juice. Bring to a boil slowly over medium heat, turn down the heat and reduce the mixture by three-fourths or until syrupy, about 30 minutes. Strain, cool, and use or store.

Curried Coconut Shrimp with Papaya-Saffron Relish
Chef Paul O'Connell

Makes 8 – 10 portions.

Ingredients

20 medium to large shrimp, peeled and deveined with tail on
3 cups shredded coconut, unsweetened
¼ cup turmeric
3 Tbsp Madras curry powder
1 tsp cinnamon
1 tsp paprika
1 tsp cumin, ground
8 egg whites lightly whisked
2 cups cornstarch
1 quart canola oil for frying
1 shallot finely minced
½ cup lemon juice
1 Tbsp saffron
2 Tbsp honey
⅛ cup red pepper, minced
⅛ cup red onion, minced
⅛ cup scallion, minced
⅛ cup cilantro, minced
Salt and pepper

Preparation

For the Shrimp
Rinse and pat dry, set aside. In a mixing bowl, toss together the coconut, turmeric, curry, cinnamon, paprika, and cumin. Set up dredging containers and fill in order with cornstarch, egg whites, and coconut mixture. Dredge the shrimp through each container and lay flat on a baking sheet. Refrigerate or freeze until ready to fry. Fry until golden in canola oil heated to 350 degrees. Set on paper towels to dry. Serve with Papaya-Saffron Relish.

For the Papaya-Saffron Relish
Place diced papaya in stainless steel mixing bowl. In a small saucepot, place the shallot, lemon juice, saffron, and honey. Heat to a simmer over moderate heat. Remove and cool. When cooled, place the saffron mixture into the papaya bowl along with the minced vegetable and toss. Adjust the seasoning with salt and pepper and check for acidity.

Plantain Crusted Red Snapper with Coconut Rice and Ahili Mohill served with Banana Chutney
Chef Paul O'Connell

Makes 6 portions.

Ingredients

2.2 lb red snapper fillet, cut in 6 oz portions
2 cups plantain chips, crushed
¼ cup flour
1 tsp cumin
Salt and pepper
1 Tbsp cilantro chopped
¼ cup canola oil

Ahili Mohill
6 garlic cloves
2 tsp cumin
Salt and pepper
2 tsp smoked Spanish paprika
½ cup red peppers, roasted and peeled
1 cup orange juice
½ cup lime juice
¼ cup extra virgin olive oil

Coconut Rice
1 ½ cups rice
3 cups water
1 bay leaf
2 oz olive oil
1 lemon cut in half
Salt to taste
¾ cup coconut milk
2 tsp canola oil
¼ cup fresh ginger, minced
¼ cup scallion, minced
⅛ cup cilantro, minced

Preparation

Place plantain chips, flour, and cumin in a food processor and pulse 3-4 times. Remove to a shallow dish large enough to dredge fish in. Season fish with salt and pepper, and rub with cilantro. Press the flesh side of the fish firmly into plantain crumb mix and repeat on skin side. Heat a sauté pan over medium heat. Add canola oil and place fish into pan flesh side down. Cook until golden (3-5 minutes) and turn over for 3 minutes on the skin side. Remove and set aside. The fish will need to cook in a 350 degree oven for 6-10 minutes. Serve with the coconut rice, Ahili Mohill sauce, and banana chutney.

For the coconut rice, add the bay leaf, olive oil, lemon, and salt to the water, and cook as directed. When the rice is done, let it cool slightly and then stir in the coconut milk, canola oil, ginger, scallion, and cilantro.

For the Ahili Mohill sauce, place the garlic, cumin, salt and pepper, paprika, roasted and peeled red peppers, orange juice, lime juice, and olive oil in a blender, and blend until smooth.

Swordfish Au Poivre with Parsnip Puree and Red Wine Braised Shallots
Chef Ken Oringer

Serves 4.

Ingredients

4 - 6 oz swordfish steaks cut into blocks 2 inches thick by 3 inches wide
2 tsp black peppercorns cracked coarsely with a rolling pin
2 tsp canola oil
1 lb parsnips
Salt and pepper to taste
1 tsp butter
12 shallots, peeled
1 cup red wine
1 tsp honey
Chervil leaves to garnish

Preparation

Peel parsnips and place in sauce pan with water.
Cook on high heat until tender and drain.
Puree in food processor with butter, pepper, and salt.

Place shallots in red wine, add honey, and cook on medium until
syrupy glazed, approximately 20 minutes. Set aside.

Preheat oven to 400 degrees.
Coat swordfish steaks with cracked pepper and salt on both sides. Heat
sauté pan with canola oil until almost smoking and add swordfish steak.
Cook until golden brown and crusty then turn. Finish cooking in oven
until fish is just cooked (+/- 8 minutes)

To Serve

Spoon parsnip puree on plate.
Place the swordfish on top and glaze with red wine shallots.
Garnish with chervil leaves and serve.

Scallops Ceviche with Watermelon, Wild Mint, and Grapefruit
Chef Ken Oringer

Ingredients

6 oz live scallops, shucked and sliced thinly
1 Tbsp lemon juice
1 Tbsp lime juice
½ Tbsp grapefruit juice
½ Tbsp lemon zest, chopped
½ Tbsp lime zest, chopped
1 pinch Chinese red pepper
10 oz grape seed oil
1 heirloom tomato, sliced into thin triangular wedges
1 seedless watermelon, cut into 1 inch cubes
3 grapefruit, peeled and segmented with pith removed
¼ cup wild mint leaves
¼ cut baby red shiso

Preparation

Slice scallops crosswise into three.

Marinate scallops in lemon juice, lime juice, grapefruit juice, zest, red pepper, salt, pepper and oil for one minute.

To Assemble

Place tomato on top of watermelon, then top with mint leaves, 2 slices of scallops, grapefruit segment, chopped zest, Chinese red pepper, and baby shiso.

Lemon – Caper Sole
Chefs Roger Berkowitz and Richard Vellante

Ingredients

1 portion (8 oz) Grey Sole
1 Tbsp seasoned flour
1 oz grape seed oil
1 oz butter melted
1 oz white cooking wine
1 ½ Tbsp butter solid
1 Tbsp capers
1 oz fresh lemon juice
1 Tbsp parsley chopped
Kosher salt and pepper to taste
1 portion jasmine rice cooked
1 lemon wheel

Preparation

Lightly flour sole. Heat a sauté pan over medium heat with 1 oz of grape seed oil and 1 oz of butter and add floured sole. Flip, finish cooking and remove from pan. Place on a dinner round.

Deglaze pan with white wine. Add capers and reduce by half.

Add COLD butter and emulsify into a butter sauce. DO NOT BOIL BUTTER. Add lemon juice and chopped parsley. Taste and adjust seasoning (salt and pepper).

Pour sauce over sole.

Place jasmine rice portion on dinner round and garnish sole with lemon wheel. Serve with a vegetable.

Baltimore Style Crab Cake
Chefs Roger Berkowitz and Richard Vellante

Ingredients

1 cup mayonnaise
1 oz Dijon mustard
2 eggs
1 oz Worcestershire sauce
2 tsp Old Bay Seasoning

2 tsp mustard powder
¼ tsp baking powder
2 lb Maryland crab
2 ½ cups Saltine crackers

Recipe yields 10 crab cakes (approximately 4 oz each)

Preparation

In a large mixing bowl combine mayonnaise, Dijon mustard, eggs, Worcestershire sauce, Tabasco, Old Bay Seasoning, mustard, and baking powder. Mix well to incorporate all ingredients. Fold in crushed saltines and crabmeat. Do not over mix. You want to see large pieces of crabmeat. Refrigerate for at least 1 hour prior to forming. Form into 4 oz loose "balls" and place on a cookie sheet.

Bake for approximately 5-7 minutes at 425 degrees.

Serve as a first course with a tablespoon of mustard sauce on the corner or as a passed appetizer with a small bowl of mustard sauce on the side.

Mustard Sauce (yields 2 ½ cups)
Ingredients

2 cups mayonnaise
2 tbsp dry mustard
½ cup heavy cream
1 Tbsp Old Bay Seasoning
1 Tbsp Worcestershire sauce
½ Tbsp chopped parsley

Preparation

Mix all ingredients together well.

Keep refrigerated until needed.

Turkish Tarator Sauce
Chef Ana Sortun

Ingredients

½ cup blanched whole almonds
½ cup eater or fish fumet
1 tsp chopped garlic
¼ cup extra virgin olive oil
Squeeze of fresh lemon
Salt and pepper to taste

Preparation

Place all ingredients in a blender (must be a blender, no substitution) and puree for at least 3 minutes until completely smooth and thick. All bits of almonds should be gone, and the sauce should be creamy and blond with a strong garlic flavor.

Top fried mussels or fried fish with the Turkish Tarator Sauce and serve with parsley and lemon.

Pan Roasted Lobster with Whiskied Honey
Chef Lydia Shire

Serves 1.

Lobster
Precook a 2 lb lobster in boiling salted water for 2 minutes.
Remove all meat from shells (tail, claws, knuckle) and set aside.

Potato Collar
Peel a potato with Japanese vegetable peeler, peel a long sheath of potato
(should be the width of a lasagna noodle). Wrap sheath around an empty soup can
(label removed and sides covered with aluminum foil). The ends of the sheath should
overlap. Secure in place with a **paper clip**. Deep fry entire can; remove potato when
golden brown. Drain on paper towel to dry and let cool to room temperature.

Whiskied Honey
Mix ½ Tbsp whiskey with 1 Tbsp of honey.

Balsamic Glaze
Reduce ¼ bottle of balsamic vinegar over medium heat until syrupy.

Spinach and Garlic
Sauté a coarsely chopped clove of garlic in olive oil a couple minutes. Add ¼ cello bag
of cleaned, fresh spinach. Season with salt and pepper. Cook uncovered quickly at
high heat; do not stir as you want the bottom side to brown.

Final Assembly
Drizzle whiskied honey and balsamic glaze – both at room temperature – on dinner
plate. Place potato collar in center of plate. Sauté lobster quickly in whole butter to
reheat. Season with salt to taste. Place warm lobster meat in potato collar, setting
aside claws for garnish.

Place warm spinach on top of lobster meat and arrange claws to peek out of
collar for garnish.

Serve immediately.

Scrod Stuffed with Shrimp and Mushrooms
Chefs Roger Berkowitz and Richard Vellante

Serves 4.

Ingredients

6 Tbsp butter
4 Tbsp minced onions
2 tsp chopped garlic
4 oz chopped mushrooms (¼ lb)
4 Tbsp dry sherry
8 oz peeled Maine shrimp or chopped gulf shrimp
2 lb scrod fillets, in 4 pieces
About ½ cup milk
½-¾ cup cracker crumb mixture

Preparation

Preheat the oven to 450 degrees. Melt 4 tablespoons of the butter in an enameled or stainless steel frying pan. Slowly cook the onions and garlic for 3 to 4 minutes. Do not let them brown. Add the mushrooms and cook for about 5 minutes, or until wilted, stirring frequently. Pour in the sherry, turn the heat to high, and cook, stirring constantly, until the sherry has been absorbed by the vegetables. Stir in the shrimp and cook, stirring constantly, for about 1 minute – just long enough to firm them slightly; the shrimp should not cook through. Set the mixture aside to cool slightly.

Dip the fish pieces into the milk and then into the cracker crumbs. Lay the fish out on the counter and center a quarter of the shrimp mixture on each piece. Fold over the ends of each piece until they meet, just covering the shrimp mixture.

Place the fish pieces, seam side down, into a buttered baking dish. The size of the dish is important – you want the fish to be closely packed but not crowded. Pat cracker crumbs over the top of each serving, pressing down slightly so the crumbs will adhere. Dot the fish with the remaining 2 tablespoons butter.

Bake for 20 to 25 minutes, or until the crumbs are browned and the fish is cooked through. Do not overcook. The fish may exude some juices; spoon them over the top before serving.

Bluefish with Mustard Sauce
Chefs Roger Berkowitz and Richard Vellante

Serves 4.

Ingredients

1½ cups mayonnaise
½ cup Dijon mustard
½ cup grated horseradish
¼ cup minced onions
¼ cup finely chopped parsley
Worcestershire sauce
Hot pepper sauce
2 lb bluefish fillets

Preparation

Preheat the oven to 450 degrees. Combine the mayonnaise, mustard, horseradish, onions and parsley. Season to taste with the Worcestershire and hot pepper sauces.

If you are baking the fish, spread it generously with the mustard sauce and bake it for 15 minutes. Should you wish to broil it, place it under a preheated broiler, and cook until almost done, about 6 minutes. Remove the fish, spread lightly with sauce, and return it under the broiler until it is lightly browned.

NOTE: Any extra sauce can be stored in the refrigerator where it is delicious with fried oysters, squid – or any broiled or baked fish.

Seared Sea Scallops with
Green Onions and Tomatoes
Chef Gordon Hamersley

Ingredients

4 large tomatoes – seeded, chopped and drained
1 Tbsp basil chopped
2 oz olive oil
1 Tbsp sherry vinegar
5 oz sea scallops per person for a main course
3 bunches scallions, cleaned, washed, and cut into 2 inch lengths
2 cloves garlic – minced
Salt and pepper
Lemon juice to taste

Preparation

To make the vinaigrette: In a mixing bowl, combine the tomatoes, basil, olive oil and a little vinegar to taste. Season with salt and pepper and let stand to blend the flavors for about 25 minutes.

Heat a skillet large enough to hold the scallops with 2 tablespoons cooking oil until very hot. Season the scallops and tomatoes with salt and pepper, and add to the pan. Cook on one side until browned. About 2 minutes. Add the garlic and green onions and toss the mixture once.

To serve

Spoon the tomato vinaigrette onto each plate and place the scallops and green onions on top.

Note: This recipe is very versatile and the main ingredient is open to many suggestions. Try chicken breast, shrimp, salmon, etc., etc.

Almond-Crusted Snapper
Chef Todd English

Here's another way to use the almondine flavors. I love the combination of the rich nuts and sharp mustard with the meaty, firm texture and sweet, strong flavor of the snapper. Serve with Saffron Risotto and Shaved Raw Fennel and Red Onion Salad.

Serves 4.

Ingredients

½ cup shelled almonds
1 bulb roasted garlic, peeled
2 Tbsp Dijon mustard
2 Tbsp virgin olive oil
1 Tbsp chopped fresh flat-leaf parsley leaves
1 tsp chopped fresh rosemary leaves or ⅓ tsp dried rosemary
1 tsp kosher salt
½ tsp black pepper
1 Tbsp olive oil
4 - 6 oz red snapper fillets, preferably Gulf Coast, scored on the skin side.

Preparation

Preheat the oven to 400 degrees.

Place the nuts in a large skillet over medium heat and cook, shaking or stirring occasionally, until the nuts are brown, about 3 to 5 minutes. Place in a food processor and pulse until ground.

Place the almonds, roasted garlic, mustard, virgin olive oil, parsley, rosemary, ½ teaspoon of the salt, and ¼ teaspoon of the pepper in a bowl, and mash to a paste. Place a large cast-iron skillet or other heavy oven proof skillet over medium-high heat and when it is hot, add the olive oil. Sprinkle the snapper with the remaining ½ teaspoon salt and ¼ teaspoon pepper. Add to the pan, skin side down, and cook until skin is crisp, about 2 minutes. Turn the fillets over and spread the top with the almond mixture. Place in oven and bake until the crust is well browned, about 6 minutes.

Serve on large platter.

Roasted Oysters
Chef Todd English

Serves 6.

Ingredients

1 Tbsp fresh lemon juice
¾ tsp lemon zest
1½ tsp balsamic vinegar
⅓ cup mascarpone cheese
2 Tbsp sour cream
¾ cup shredded radicchio leaves
3 scallions, cut lengthwise
18 – 24 fresh oysters, shucked
1 tsp kosher salt
¼ - ½ tsp black pepper

Preparation

Preheat the broiler.
Place the lemon juice, zest, balsamic vinegar, mascarpone cheese, and sour cream in a small bowl and mix to combine. Fold in radicchio and scallions.
Line a decorative baking pan with rock salt and seaweed. Place oysters on the pan and top with heaping tablespoons of the mascarpone mixture.
Broil until the mascarpone turns golden brown, about 3-4 minutes.
Do not overcook.

Caciuccio-Tuscan Fish Stew
Chef Jimmy Burke

Serves 4-6 people.

Ingredients

2 Tbsp chopped parsley
¼ cup olive oil
4 Tbsp extra virgin olive oil for finishing
¼ loaf Italian or French bread
6 cloves garlic sliced
1 Spanish onion sliced
½ bulb fresh fennel
1 tsp crushed red pepper
2 cups canned tomatoes chopped
2 stalks celery chopped
1 gallon fish stock
16 littleneck clams cleaned
16 medium shrimp peeled and deveined
2 lb cleaned monkfish cut into large chunks
24 mussels cleaned
1 lobster 1-¼ lb

Preparation

Boil the lobster for 4-5 minutes and cool in refrigerator. In a heavy bottomed pot, sauté the vegetables in the olive oil until tender. Add the fish stock and simmer slowly for 30 minutes. While soup base is cooking, clean the fish and shell fish, cut the lobster in quarters, clean the head and crack the shells. Cut the bread on the bias and brush with olive oil, and set aside (if you have a grill, get it hot). Strain the soup base. At this point, you can either continue or cool the soup base for later use.

Have your soup base hot while you start to prepare the finished product. The important thing in this preparation is the sequence in which you cook the fish. Place the pot with soup base on a high heat, make sure it comes to a boil. Add the clams first and cover. When the clams look like they are beginning to open, add the monkfish, and cook for two minutes. Add the lobster, then the mussels and shrimp. When they are all cooked, grill the bread and place in a deep bowl. Sort out equal portions of fish and shellfish, season the broth with salt and pepper, add the extra virgin olive oil, and cover each bowl of fish and shellfish with the broth. Garnish with chopped parsley and serve.

If a grill is not available, you may sauté bread in olive oil.

Vivo Restaurant Maine Lobster Fettuccine with Sweet Corn and Basil Butter
Chef Jimmy Burke

This is a summer dish that is a favorite of mine, having lived in New England my whole life and being able to get the best lobsters from Maine, fresh local corn and basil from the garden. The basil butter and cooked corn can be done a day in advance if necessary.

Ingredients

4 one lb lobsters
1 lb fresh or good quality dry egg noodle, (fettuccine will do)
3 ears fresh corn
Salt and pepper
2 sticks butter – either salted or unsalted, just adjust seasoning accordingly
½ cup basil
Coarse salt and pepper

Preparation

Basil butter
Soften butter at room temperature, then combine basil and butter in a food processor, puree until smooth, add salt and pepper to taste, then either roll the butter in wax paper, or place in a container in refrigerator.

Corn
Peel and boil the corn in lightly salted water for 5 minutes, cool, and remove from cob. Save the water and use it to cook the pasta.

Lobster Fettucine
Boil lobsters for 5 minutes, cool, and remove meat from shell. Split the tails and when ready, sauté gently in 3 tablespoons of butter, add corn and continue to cook for two minutes. Cook pasta according to directions on box, drain, and toss in with lobster and corn, take half the basil butter and toss in with lobster pasta mixture, use more if necessary and serve.

Marinated Salmon in Muscadet
Chef Andreé Robert

Serves 6.

Ingredients

1 skinless, boneless salmon fillet, approximately 2 lb
1 bottle Muscadet wine
½ cup lemon juice
½ cup freshly snipped chives
Freshly ground black pepper, salt (to taste)

Preparation

A long sharp knife is needed. Set the salmon on a board so the tail is closest to
the hand holding the knife at a 45 degree angle. Cut the salmon into ⅛ inch slices,
beginning at the tail. Put one layer on a large non-aluminum roasting pan. Sprinkle
slices well with wine, lemon juice, chives, and pepper. Continue to layer and add
marinade until everything is used. Cover pan tightly with plastic wrap; refrigerate
for 24 hours. Rotate slices so they marinate evenly. Use a large metal spatula to lift
slices of salmon from pan. Arrange in a fan-like shape on salad plates. Sprinkle
with extra chives. Serve with slices of dark, dense rye bread.

Pacific Northwest Dungeness Crab Ravioli with Thyme-Tomato Broth

Chef Jamie Mammano

Serves 4.

Ingredients

Ravioli
1 each Dungeness Crab (live if possible)
about 2 lb cooked and cleaned;
reserving shell and meat separately
(about 8 ounces of meat)
16 each wonton skins
¼ cup Mascarpone cheese
2 Tbsp grated Parmesan cheese
¼ cup finely chopped chives
Salt and pepper
1 egg (beaten for egg wash)

Broth
2 cups chicken broth
1 cup dry white wine
1 cup Mirepoix (fine chopped
onion, carrot, and celery)
Sprig thyme
Pinch salt
Reserved crab shells

Garnish
2 tbsp chopped chives
¼ cup finely diced tomato 2
Tbsp whole butter
Pinch thyme

Preparation

Cook Dungeness Crab in boiling sea salted water as you would for a similar sized lobster (approx. 18 minutes). Quickly cool crab in ice water bath and remove. Break apart and carefully remove all meat from crab shell. Save shells for the broth.

For Ravioli
In chilled bowl place crabmeat, cheeses and chives, and fold together. Season with salt and pepper to taste. Lay out a few wonton skins at a time, brush egg wash lightly on ½ of surface area and place 1 tablespoon of crab filling on each of the skins, fold over and press edges firmly together to form ravioli, continue until 16 pieces are done, reserve ravioli in refrigerator.

For Crab Broth
Combine crab shells, white wine, chicken broth, mirepoix, thyme, and salt in small sauce pot, cover and simmer for 30 minutes. Strain first through strainer and strain through a coffee filter a second time to obtain a clear broth. Reserve.

To Serve
Bring crab broth to simmer, simultaneously cook ravioli in boiling salted water for 2½ - 3 minutes, strain and distribute the ravioli into 4 soup plates, add tomato, chive, thyme, and butter to hot crab broth. Spoon evenly amongst 4 bowls of ravioli and serve.

Halibut with Wild Mushrooms and Truffle Vinaigrette
Chef Michael Schlow

Makes 2 middle courses

Ingredients
2-4 oz pieces of halibut fillet
1 cup assorted wild mushrooms
1 large shallot peeled and quartered
2 Tbsp truffle vinaigrette (recipe to follow)
2 Tbsp carrot juice reduction
Olive oil
Salt and pepper
Fresh thyme
Lemon juice

Truffle Vinaigrette
3 Tbsp reduced balsamic vinegar
1 minced shallot
Pinch chopped thyme
10 Tbsp Truffle oil
Salt, pepper, and chives

Combine all ingredients but do not mix well

Carrot Reduction
1 cup carrot juice
Reduce by ⅔, season with salt and sugar, pinch of curry

Preparation

Before you begin this dish, first make the carrot juice reduction and the truffle vinaigrette. You'll need two sauté pans. First for the fish, heat one sauté pan with a little olive oil. Season the fish with salt and pepper. Gently sear the fish until golden brown on one side. Flip the fish and baste with a pinch of thyme. Cook for about 2 minutes on each side. Deglaze with lemon juice. In the other pan, sauté the mushrooms and shallots in 1 tsp. of butter and 1 oz. of olive oil. Sauté for 2 minutes, add thyme and lemon juice. Place the mushroom mixture in the center of two plates, top with the fish and spoon some of the vinaigrette around the plate. Place a few drops of the carrot reduction around the plate as well, garnish with some fresh herbs and serve.

Simple Grilled Swordfish Skewers
Chef Chris Schlesinger

Swordfish is excellent for grilling and particularly good for kebobs because of its firm texture. Here we kept it simple – just rub the fish with a spice herb mixture, thread it onto the skewers with some onion chunks, and grill it up. This goes very nicely with rice pilaf (use boxed rice pilaf if you want), simply pile some pilaf on each plate and slide the fish off the skewers on top. If you want to dress up the skewers a bit, cut a couple of nectarines into quarters and add two quarters to each skewer.

Ingredients

1 lb swordfish, cut into 1-inch chunks (about 12 chunks)
2 small red onions, peeled and cut into eighths
2 tablespoons olive oil
1 lemon, quartered

For the Rub

3 Tbsp olive oil
3 Tbsp cumin seeds, toasted if you want, or 1½ Tbsp ground cumin
1 Tbsp minced garlic
¼ cup roughly chopped fresh oregano or parsley
2 tsp salt
2 tsp freshly cracked pepper

Preparation

Make the rub; in a small bowl, combine all the ingredients and mix well.

Thread the swordfish and red onions alternately onto skewers and sprinkle with spice rub. Place the skewers on the grill over medium-hot fire and cook for 7 minutes on each side, or until a peek inside shows that the fish is opaque all the way through. Remove from the fire, sprinkle with olive oil, serve with lemon wedges for squeezing.

Summer Striped Bass Salad
Chef Chris Schlesinger

I'm lucky enough to be able to spend time at the beach in southern Massachusetts in the summer, and sometimes I'm even fortunate enough to catch some fish down there. If I don't, I can always go on over to the local fish store, which buys the catch of small fishermen. Seeing that this area is big striped bass hangout, and being that striper in my humble opinion is one of the finest eating fish in the universe (along with pompano and red snapper), I have had the occasion to grill many a striped bass, which means I sometimes have leftovers to use up the next day. So I took the Southeast Asian idea of salads made of fish tossed with lime and herbs and added the smokiness of grilling to boost the flavor dynamism. If you don't have striped bass, you can make this with snapper, tuna, monkfish, swordfish, halibut – or just about any fish or seafood that you can grill. (Serves 4.)

Ingredients

1 lb striped bass fillets, skinned and any bones removed (or last night's leftover grilled fish)
2 Tbsp olive oil
Salt and freshly cracked black pepper to taste
1 large tomato, cored and diced medium
1 small red onion, peeled and thinly sliced
½ cup thinly sliced scallions (white and green parts)
¼ cup roughly chopped fresh basil
¼ cup roughly chopped fresh mint
⅓ cup fresh lime juice (about 2 large limes)
1 Tbsp minced ginger
4-6 dashes Tabasco sauce

Preparation

Rub the bass lightly with the olive oil, sprinkle with salt and pepper to taste, and grill over a medium-hot fire for 5-7 minutes per side. To check for doneness: cut into one of the pieces of fish and check to see that is just opaque throughout.

Remove the fish from the grill and as soon as it is cool enough to handle, flake the meat from the skin with a fork. The meat will be tossed in with the salad, so don't worry if it comes off in small pieces.

Place the fish in a medium sauce bowl, add all remaining ingredients, and season to taste with salt and pepper. Toss lightly and serve. This salad will keep, covered and refrigerated, for 2-3 days.

Scallop and Nectarine Skewers
with Grilled Red Pepper – Lime Sauce
Chef Chris Schlesinger

Serves 4 as an entrée or 8 as an appetizer.

Scallops on the grill are super easy if you firm them up with a quick blanch first. In this case we skewer the blanched scallops with nectarines, which take on a slight char by the time the scallops are cooked through. Then we finish off the dish with a smoky sauce heavy on grilled peppers and lime juice. This makes a colorful dish for a summer lunch.

Ingredients

2 lb (20-30) medium size sea scallops (about the size of pinball balls)
4 nectarines, peeled and cut into 8 wedges (you may substitute peaches)

Sauce
1 large yellow onion, sliced ½ inch thick
3 red bell peppers, halved
2 Tbsp vegetable oil
1 garlic clove
½ cup chicken stock
¼ cup lime juice (about 2 limes)
¼ cup chopped fresh cilantro
Pinch red pepper flakes
Salt and freshly cracked black pepper to taste
¼ cup virgin olive oil

Preparation

Make the sauce: Rub the onion slices and bell pepper halves lightly with vegetable oil and grill over a medium-hot fire until golden brown, 3-4 minutes per side. Remove from the grill. In a food processor or blender, combine the grilled peppers and onions with all the remaining sauce ingredients except the olive oil and puree. With the food processor or blender still running, add the olive oil in a steady stream. Set the sauce aside.

Grill the skewers: Blanch the scallops in boiling water for 1 minute, drain, and sprinkle with salt and pepper. Thread the scallops onto skewers alternately with pieces of nectarine. You should have about 8 skewers.

Over a medium-hot fire, grill the skewers for 2-3 minutes per side, or until the scallops are light brown on the outside and just opaque throughout. Serve with the red pepper-lime sauce.

Linguine with Lobster in Lemon Parsley Sauce
Chef Michela Larson

Ingredients

1 shallot minced
1 packed cup of parsley coarsely chopped
3 Tbsp more of parsley for garnish
1 lb linguine
Juice of one lemon
Finely grated zest of one lemon
1¼ lb cooked lobster meat, cut in 1-inch chunks
3 Tbsp garlic oil (see below)
8 oz Mascarpone cheese
1 Tbsp hot red pepper flakes (optional and to taste)

Garlic oil
1 cup extra virgin olive oil
10 cloves of garlic, peeled and smashed
1 handful small-leaf basil

Preparation

In a small saucepan, warm the oil on low heat with garlic cloves. In a few minutes, bubbles will begin to appear. Keep a close eye and don't let the oil boil. Stir frequently for about 10 minutes, then remove from heat. Once cooled, add basil leaves. Garlic oil can be stored in glass container in fridge for a couple of weeks.

Lobster
Already cooked fresh lobster meat can be purchased from your local purveyor. Make sure that you are getting all parts if you do so—tails, claws, knuckles. Cut the pieces into the 1- inch chunks.

If you are cooking lobster fresh, you will need 4-6 1¼ lb lobsters to get 1¼ lb cooked lobster meat. Bring a large pot of salted water (2 **tablespoons** of salt to every quart of water) to a rolling boil. Cook lobsters in batches. Don't crowd. Once water has returned to rolling boil, cook for 5 minutes. Cool slightly, then remove lobster meat from shell, and cut into 1-inch chunks. Toss the lobster with the cup of parsley and the grated zest of lemon. Set aside.

And Pasta

Cook the pasta until it is not quite done. It should still be very chewy as it will be cooked once more with the lobster. Drain, toss with half the garlic oil, and save 1 cup of the pasta water.

In a large sauté pan—big enough to hold both pasta and lobster, heat half of the garlic oil and lightly sauté the minced shallot until just softened. Add the pasta, the lobster, lemon juice, and optional red pepper flakes, and stir together carefully. Add pasta water slowly as needed. Keep stirring and add 4 oz. of the Mascarpone in portions so that it can get incorporated. Once all is heated through (be careful not to overcook), taste for seasoning. Add salt and pepper as needed.

Serve immediately—making sure everyone gets their fair share of lobster. Sprinkle a bit more chopped parsley over the dish and add a small dollop of Mascarpone in the center.

Ms. Annie's Fried Shrimps
Chef Michelle White

If you love shrimp this simple recipe will become your go-to recipe in a pinch. Fried to perfection. Great as an appetizer or meal. Serves 5.

Ingredients

Shrimp (16-20) 2 lb peeled, cleaned, and deveined
Salt, pepper, your favorite seasonings
½ cup whole milk
1 cup corn flour
4 cup all-purpose flour
Cast iron or any shallow frying pan half filled with corn oil

Preparation

Peel, wash and devein shrimp.
Add seasonings and milk. Be careful with seasoning; shrimp are naturally seasoned by the salt in sea water. Let stand at least 30 minutes.

Mix corn flour and all-purpose flour. Coat shrimp with flour mixture and shake off excess.

Fry shrimp in batches 8 to 10 pieces at a time. Take your time and fry until slightly tan and remove, place on paper towels to drain oil (**first** batch).

Watch oil temperature then fry 8 to 10 pieces more (**second** batch).

Place **first** batch back in oil and cook until golden but not dark brown. Shrimp take no time to cook.

Add **second** batch until finished.

Poultry

Oliver's Chicken Stew with Lemon Tarragon, Parmesan Cheese, and Tiny Pasta
Chef Jody Adams

Serves 4.

Ingredients

5 cups chicken broth
Salt and freshly ground pepper
1 small carrot, peeled and cut into julienne
1 stalk celery, peeled and cut into julienne
1 leek, white part only, washed and cut into julienne
1 tsp garlic, minced
2 Tbsp chopped fresh tarragon
2 boneless chicken breasts, thinly sliced
2 Tbsp stellette or other tiny pasta
4 squash blossoms (optional)
2-3 Tbsp freshly squeezed lemon juice
4 Tbsp unsalted butter
4 half-inch slices rustic bread, grilled or toasted and rubbed with extra virgin olive oil
¼ cup grated Parmesan cheese
2 Tbsp chopped fresh parsley
4 parsley sprigs

Preparation

Heat the broth in a large pot. Season with salt and pepper. Add the vegetables and chicken breasts and poach over moderate heat, 5-6 minutes or until done. Remove and set aside. Add the pasta and cook until done, about 10 minutes. Scoop out the pasta and set aside. When cool enough to handle, stuff a teaspoon or so of the pasta into each of the squash blossoms.
Add the tarragon, lemon juice, and butter to the broth and taste for seasoning. It should have a pronounced tarragon and lemon flavor. Return the vegetables, chicken, and remaining pasta to the broth and warm through.

Place a slice of toasted bread into each of four warmed bowls. Cover with a tablespoon of Parmesan cheese. Ladle the stew over the bread. Set squash blossom on top. Garnish with chopped parsley sprigs. Serve immediately.

Chicken Boudin
Chef Frank McClelland

Ingredients

1 lb chicken breasts and legs, boneless and skinless
3 eggs separated
1 carrot, diced small
1 rib celery, diced small
2 shallots, diced small
2 cloves garlic, minced
¼ cup spinach, cooked and chopped
¼ lb wild mushrooms, cooked and chopped
¼ cup chestnuts, sliced
1 tsp salt

Zest of 1 lemon
1¼ cups heavy cream
White pepper
Cayenne pepper
Nutmeg
Fresh thyme
Salt and pepper to taste
1 gallon chicken broth
½ cup cornmeal

Preparation

Sweat and cool diced vegetables. Grind meat in food processor until smooth, wiping down the sides of the bowl with a rubber spatula. Gradually add egg whites while mixture is grinding. Add yolks and continue to grind until smooth. Scrape into the mixing bowl of an electric mixer. Allow to cool over ice until the mixture reaches 38 degrees. Once it has cooled, place in machine and begin mixing using the whisk attachment. Add salt and mix at a high speed for 45 seconds until it develops a sheen. At a lower speed gradually add heavy cream. Add seasonings while whisking.

Remove from mixer and with a rubber spatula fold in sweated, diced vegetables, spinach, chestnuts, and mushrooms. Spoon the mixture in the form of a 2-inch log onto the center of large piece of cellophane. Lengthwise, fold the top of the cellophane towards you keeping the mixture tightly wrapped by using your hand as a wedge. Holding both ends, roll the cellophane creating a tight log. Tie each end of cellophane in a knot. Poach boudin in simmering chicken broth until it reaches an internal temperature of 140 degrees.

Remove from broth and shock in ice water, until boudin is fully cool. Remove from cellophane and roll in mixture of cornmeal, salt and pepper. In a pan, sauté boudin in oil over a high flame until golden brown.

Warmed Roquefort Flan with Duck Salad
Chef Mary-Catherine Deibel

Roquefort Flan

4 Tbsp. fine bread crumbs
2 Tbsp. clarified butter
2 cups cream cheese
2 cups sour cream
½ cup heavy cream
2 cups Roquefort (less if desired)
small amount of lemon juice

Fresh thyme
Freshly cracked black pepper
8 six oz ramekins
Food processor

Place Roquefort in the bowl of the food processor. Pulse on and off to break up. Add cream cheese, sour cream, lemon juice, thyme, and black pepper. Thin with heavy cream.

Lightly grease the ramekins with clarified butter. Dust with bread crumbs. Add flan mixture. Place ramekins in a water bath and bake at 350 degrees for one hour.

Keep at room temperature until ready to serve.

Dressing

2 cups extra virgin olive oil
⅔ cup raspberry vinegar
3 Tbsp. honey
2 cloves garlic
Finely chopped rosemary
Coarse salt **and** freshly ground pepper to taste

Mix all ingredients with a whisk.

Duck Salad

4 duck breasts (can be purchased already butchered), seared and sautéed to rare, cut into thin slices.

½ sautéed pancetta or Cobb bacon

2 cups cooked white or cranberry beans

½ cup pitted Calamata olives

½ cup purple onion, finely diced

1 cup fresh orange sections (membranes removed, each section halved)

Fresh bitter organic greens (good with young dandelion greens in the spring, with frisee and mache in other seasons)

Fresh sage leaves, deep-fried in clarified butter and very lightly salted.

To Assemble Warmed Roquefort Flan with Duck Salad

Dress greens lightly and place on 10-inch plate. Scatter white beans, pancetta or bacon, olives, onions, and orange sections on greens.

Remove warmed flan from ramekins and place in the middle of the plate of greens. Surround with a fan of thinly sliced rare duck breasts.

Garnish with deep-fried sage leaves

This recipe will serve eight, allowing ½ duck breast per person, as a first course, or four as a main course. The salad can also be served with seared pheasant breast instead of duck breast.

Chicken with Brined Vegetables (Gardiniera)
Chef Moncef Meddeb

Ingredients

16 oz boneless, skinless chicken breasts
3 or 4 oz brined vegetables
3 oz olives (green)
1 ½ Serano chilis (or 2 dehydrated chipotles)
3 oz cooked white beans
⅔ oz capers
1 onion (diced)
A few sprigs of cilantro
Rind of lemon cooked in salt water
2 Tbsp olive oil
1 Tbsp tomato paste
½ Tbsp harissa or chili paste
½ Tbsp paprika
½ Tbsp coriander
Salt and pepper to taste

Preparation

Cut chicken breasts in half. Set cooking dish over high heat, add olive oil, diced onion, and chicken breasts. Lightly brown, reduce heat to simmer, add tomato paste, harissa, paprika, and a little water.

Add salt, pepper, coriander, and lemon. Simmer 10 minutes, add minced brined vegetables, beans, chilies, capers, and olives.

Cook 10 to 15 minutes. Serve and garnish with fresh coriander (cilantro).

Curried Spaghetti with Roast Capon, Pinenuts and Raisins
Chef Daniele Baliani

Ingredients

1 whole capon or 1 large 6 lb roaster
4 heads of garlic, split in half
2 large onions, cut in wide strips
2 medium carrots, roughly chopped
1 tsp chile flakes
6 Tbsp of high quality curry powder
¼ cup of olive oil

For the Garnish
Carved slices of capon breast Fried
mint leaves (optional)
Curry oil (optional)

1 cup of white wine
2 quarts of chicken stock
½ cup of heavy cream
1 cup golden raisins
1 Tbsp butter
1 Tbsp of Parmesan cheese
¼ cup toasted pinenuts
Salt and pepper to taste

Preparation

Roasting the breast

Pre-heat your oven to 450 degrees. Begin by separating the capon into wings, thighs, drumsticks, and breast cavity (only wings and legs are used for the sauce). Make a paste by combining 3 tablespoons of extra virgin olive oil with 1 tablespoon of curry powder. Rub the breast cavity inside and out with the paste, and season with salt and pepper. Place the breast cavity in the oven and roast at 450 degrees for approximately 15 minutes. Lower the heat to 350 degrees and continue roasting for approximately 30 minutes more. Set aside to cool slightly, then carve into thin slices for garnishing the plates.

Making the sauce

While the breast is roasting, place the wings, thighs, and drumsticks in a 4-quart casserole. Over medium heat, brown the capon pieces with 2 tablespoons of olive oil. When the skin has browned on all sides, remove the pieces from the pan, and pour off any excess fat drippings. Return the pieces to the pan and add garlic, onions, and carrots. Allow the vegetables to sweat and caramelize slightly with the capon pieces. Sprinkle 4 tablespoons of curry powder and the chile flakes over the whole mixture and continue caramelizing until everything is golden brown and just starting to stick to the bottom of the pan. Deglaze with the white wine and when the liquid has evaporated, add enough chicken stock to barely cover the capon and vegetables. Bring to a simmer and braise for approximately 30 minutes, adding the heavy cream halfway through the cooking to bind and enrichen the sauce. Remove the capon pieces and strain the sauce through a china cap. When the capon pieces have cooled, pull the meat off the bones & add back to the sauce. Season to taste.

To complete the dish
Fill a 2-gallon stockpot ¾ full of water and bring to a boil. Season the water with 1 cup of salt and plunge the spaghetti into the rolling boil, stirring quickly to keep the strands from clumping. While pasta cooks, place a large skillet over a medium heat. Add the sauce and capon pieces and bring to a simmer. Add the raisins and cook 2-3 minutes until they are plump. At this time, the spaghetti should be cooked "al dente." Drain directly into the sauce and toss with butter and Parmesan cheese. Finish by sprinkling toasted pinenuts as well as thin slices of capon breast. For a fancier presentation, top with fried mint leaves and drizzle curry oil.

Buon Appetito!!!

Foie Gras and Black Truffle Flan with Wild Mushroom Ragu and Mache
Chef Todd English

This is an ultimate indulgence, to be enjoyed when your budget, either caloric or cash, is not a consideration. Unbelievably rich and intense, yet somehow also light and smooth, this flan is a perfect starter to any steak dish. Serves 4.

Ingredients

2 cups heavy cream
4 oz raw foie gras, finely chopped (available at specialty food shops or by mail order)
1 oz fresh, canned, or frozen black truffle
5 large egg yolks
1 tsp kosher salt
½ tsp black pepper
1 tsp truffle oil (optional)

Wild Mushroom Ragu
1 Tbsp unsalted butter
⅓ to ¾ lb assorted mushrooms, such as shiitake, portobello, hedgehog, and/or yellow-foot chanterelles, trimmed and wiped clean
1 shallot, diced
1 Tbsp red wine or ruby port
1 cup chicken broth, dark stock, or canned low-sodium chicken broth
1 tsp fresh thyme leaves
½ tsp kosher salt
¼ tsp black pepper
4 bunches mache (lamb's lettuce) or 4 sprigs chervil

Preparation

Preheat the oven to 325 degrees. Butter four ¾ –cup flan or soufflé molds. Place ½ cup of the cream and the foie gras in a blender or food processor and process until just blended. Pass the mixture through a fine strainer into a stainless steel bowl. Discard the solids.

Place ½ cup of the cream and the truffles in the food processor or blender and process briefly. Transfer to the bowl with the foie gras. Add the remaining 1 cup cream, the egg yolks, salt, pepper, and, if desired, the truffle oil, and blend well until well incorporated. Pour into the prepared molds and place in a larger pan filled with enough water to come halfway up the sides of the molds. Bake until the flans are firm to the touch, about 45 minutes.

To make the ragu
Melt the butter in a large skillet over medium heat. Add the mushrooms and shallot and cook until the mushrooms are golden and tender, about 10 minutes. Add the wine and scrape the browned bits from the bottom of the pan. Add the stock, thyme, salt and pepper, and simmer until reduced to a saucelike consistency, about 10 minutes.

To serve
Divide the ragu among four plates, spreading the mushrooms out evenly. Carefully unmold the flan on top of the ragu by running a knife around the sides. Garnish each plate with the mache or chervil. Serve warm.

Brioche Stuffing
Chef Frank McClelland

Ingredients

2 Tbsp butter
2 Tbsp olive oil
1 each large Spanish onion, diced
2 ribs celery, diced
2 each garlic cloves, minced
3 each Cortland or Granny Smith Apples, peeled and diced
1 Tbsp sage, dried
1 tsp tarragon, dried
1 tsp thyme, dried
2 cups cranberries, dried
6 cups brioche crumbs
1 ½ cups chicken or vegetable stock, hot
Salt and pepper

Preparation

Place a large skillet over low heat. Add the olive oil and butter to the skillet, then melt the butter. Add onions, celery, garlic, and apples to the skillet, stirring occasionally with a wooden spoon. Continue cooking over low heat until the onions are transparent. Add the dried herbs, cranberries, and brioche crumbs. Continue to cook until the crumbs begin to brown, stirring often. Gradually stir in stock. Season with salt and pepper. Serve immediately or cool in a shallow pan and stuff into a bird.

As an option, omit the butter and oil, and start by browning ½ lb sausage in the skillet, then follow the above recipe.

To make brioche crumbs
Dice brioche loaves and dry overnight or toast the bread in an oven. Grind the bread to crumbs in a food processor.

Peach and Chicken Skewers with Middle Eastern Shake and Simple Raisin Sauce
Chef Chris Schlesinger

The idea for the "shake" that I use in this dish came from the Rendezvous restaurant in Memphis, Tennessee, where Charlie Vergo sets out salt shakers of his secret barbeque rub on the table so you can add it to barbecued baby back ribs. If you can double or triple the recipe for the simple shake used here, you can do the same for your guests. When you are cooking on skewers, it is crucial always to check the food for doneness before you take it off the grill. If you pack the food onto the skewers too tightly, it may not cook through in the estimated time…a particular downer when the skewered food is chicken, because most people are really not into rare chicken.

Ingredients for the Raisin Sauce
⅓ cup olive oil
¼ cup raisins, roughly chopped
⅗ cup fresh lime juice (about 2 limes)
Salt and freshly cracked black pepper to taste

Ingredients for the Shake
2 Tbsp cumin seeds, toasted if you want, or 1 tablespoon ground cumin
2 Tbsp ground coriander, toasted along with the cumin seeds if you want
Pinch of ground cinnamon
1 Tbsp kosher salt
1 Tbsp freshly cracked black pepper
3 Tbsp vegetable oil
1 Tbsp minced garlic
¼ cup roughly chopped fresh cilantro
Salt and freshly cracked pepper to taste
1 lb boneless, skinless chicken breasts, cut into large chunks (about 16 chunks)
2 red bell peppers, halved, seeded, and halves quartered
2 peaches, pitted and cut into eighths

Preparation
Make the sauce in a small bowl, combine all the ingredients. Whisk together well and set aside. Make the shake in a small bowl, combine all the ingredients, mix well, and set aside. In medium bowl, combine the oil, garlic, cilantro, and salt and pepper to taste. Add the chicken chunks and toss well so the chicken becomes well coated. Thread the chicken onto 4 skewers alternately with the peaches and pepper pieces, place the skewers on the grill over a medium fire, and cook for 5 to 7 minutes per side. To check for doneness, cut into one of the pieces of chicken and check to be sure it is opaque all the way through.

Korean-Style Grilled Chicken Wings
Chef Chris Schlesinger

I'm a big fan of wings. They don't take long to grill, they have a high ratio of crisp skin (my favorite) to meat, and, best of all, you get to eat with your hands. I like to grill the wings and then toss them with a sauce, in this case a hoisin based sauce with lots of Korean flavors. Serves 4 to 6.

Ingredients

1 Tbsp vegetable oil
½ white onion, peeled and diced small
2 Tbsp minced garlic
3 Tbsp minced ginger
2 Tbsp minced fresh chile pepper of your choice (optional)
½ red bell pepper, seeded and diced small.
½ cup hoisin sauce
¼ cup fresh lime juice (about 2 limes)
30 chicken wings
Salt and freshly cracked white pepper to taste (or substitute black pepper)
¼ cup roughly chopped fresh basil

Preparation

In a small saucepan over medium heat, heat the oil until hot but not smoking. Add the onion and sauté, stirring occasionally, until transparent, 5 to 7 minutes. Add the garlic, ginger and chile, if you're using it, and sauté, stirring occasionally for 1 minute. Add the bell peppers and sauté, stirring occasionally until soft, about 3 minutes. Stir in the hoisin sauce and lime juice, bring to a simmer gently for 5 minutes, stirring every once in a while. Remove from heat and set aside.

Separate the chicken wings into three sections each by cutting through both joints. Reserve the tips for making stock. Sprinkle the wings sections with salt and pepper to taste and grill over a medium hot fire, turning occasionally, until golden brown, about 5 minutes. To check for doneness, cut into one of the thicker wings and check to be sure it is opaque all the way through.

Remove the wings from the grill and place in a medium bowl. Add the sauce and basil, toss, and serve immediately.

Roasted Chicken Legs Mediterranean
Chef Michela Larson

Ingredients

2 Tbsp capers rinsed
½ cup oil-cured black olives
1 medium shallot sliced in thin rounds
1 Tbsp hot red chile flakes
¼ cup chopped fresh herbs: thyme, rosemary, oregano
1 medium fennel sliced
1 packed full cup of slow-roasted tomatoes (see recipe below—make the day before)
4 garlic cloves smashed
8-10 baby artichoke hearts, sliced in half
4 chicken legs trimmed of excess fat, seasoned lightly with salt & pepper

Slow-Roasted Tomatoes
15 medium plum tomatoes cut in half top to stem
Olive oil
Salt and pepper
6 cloves of garlic, smashed
Large handful of basil leaves

Preparation

The Slow-Roasted Tomatoes
Preheat oven to 225. Place tomatoes cut side down on well-oiled sheet pan. Sprinkle with salt and pepper. Roast for 3 hours. For last half hour, raise heat to 250. Let cool then store in glass container, layering in the basil leaves and crushed garlic. Pour olive oil over all until covered. These can be refrigerated and stored for up to 2 weeks.

The Chicken
Preheat oven to 425. In a roasting pan large enough to hold the 4 legs comfortably, strew around half of the capers, half of the olives, and half of the cut shallots. Layer in the smashed garlic, about two-thirds of the cut fennel, slow-roasted tomatoes, and artichoke hearts. Combine chile flakes with herbs and sprinkle about half over the vegetable base. Sprinkle salt and pepper. Add the seasoned chicken legs skin side up, leaving enough room between each so that you can tuck in the rest of the vegetables. Once you have placed the tomatoes, fennel and artichoke hearts around the chicken, add the remainder of the capers, olives and shallots. Finally, sprinkle the remaining herbs and chile flakes over all. Drizzle all with olive oil. (You may want to use some of the flavored oil from the roasted tomatoes.) Roast on the middle rack in the oven for approximately 45 minutes to one hour. You want the chicken browned and crispy. I serve the chicken with forbidden rice.

Baked Turkey Wings with Vegetables and Country Gravy
Chef Michelle White

This recipe is what I like to call 'Soul Food Sunday Dinner worthy!' because it just feels like something special to cook when you have a little extra time. Now you can have this delicious slice of heaven any day of the week. Serves 5-7.

Ingredients

2 turkey wings (medium size)
2 turkey drumsticks (small size)
1 large onion
1 small green bell pepper
1 small red pepper
1 small yellow or orange pepper
2-3 Tbsp of cornstarch to add to juices from baking turkey
Liquids: Save from baked turkey
3 cups broth- Add cornstarch
Season to taste with salt & pepper. If you like a little kick just add crushed pepper flakes and garlic cloves.

Preparation

Wash and cut turkey wings and/or drumsticks into desired pieces or leave whole (I like them whole) then season turkey pieces. Cut vegetables into 1 inch cubes and place in a bowl. Place turkey in a full-sized aluminum tray or glass baking pan at least 9x13 inch. Cover with top or foil. Place in oven and bake for 1 hour at 425 degrees.

Remove from oven, drain juices into a bowl then add cornstarch to juices. Be careful it's hot! Add vegetables, then cornstarch mixture over turkey and vegetables. Make sure gravy juices almost cover the turkey pieces/parts. Place back in oven uncovered and cook until tender, brown and bubbly. Enjoy!

Triple S Chicken: Sweet, Spicy, and Smokey Grilled Chicken
Chef Michelle White

This recipe really comes in handy when you want to turn it up a little bit on a week day. Use what you have or just your favorite parts of a chicken (10-12 pieces). Grill it or bake it uncovered in the oven.

Ingredients

10-12 pieces of chicken
3 cups of your favorite sweet BBQ sauce
¼ cup vinegar
1-2 Tbsp Liquid Smoke (optional)
1 cup pineapple juice or your favorite fruit juice
½ cup brown sugar
3 Tbsp crushed garlic
Red pepper flakes
Salt, pepper, garlic powder
Your favorite seasonings to taste.

Preparation

Combine sugar, salt and pepper, garlic powder, red pepper flakes, liquid smoke, vinegar, and crushed garlic with fruit juice. Mix and place in bowl. Set aside. Wash chicken and dry. Set chicken in a large bowl. Add sweet spice mix to chicken, massage it and let it sit in covered bowl at least 24 hours. Yes, a whole day to marinate. Don't worry, it's so worth the wait! If needed, dry off pieces with paper towel, and then place on a half sheet pan lined with parchment paper. Place chicken pieces an inch apart.

If using the oven, bake chicken at 425 degrees for 40 minutes or until clear juices run out of the chicken pieces. Remove from oven and brush on the sweet BBQ sauce. Place back in oven until the Triple S chicken becomes bubbly and sticky. Remove and serve.

If using the grill, prepare grill (hot-heated side/cooler side). Place chicken pieces on hot side for 20 minutes, then move to cooler side with grill cover down, and cook until clear juices run out of chicken. Add sweet BBQ with brush and cover chicken for last 10 minutes. Serve and enjoy.

Meats

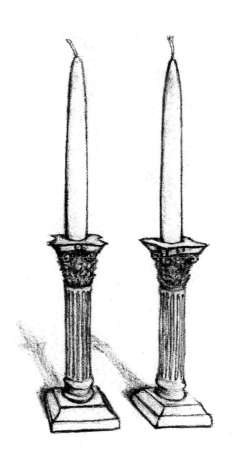

MIDA Steak and Potatoes
Chef Douglass Williams

"Julia had a spirit and ambition that initially caught people by surprise. These traits were so important as she broke barriers in the kitchen and restaurant industry. I know from my own experiences you need both of those characteristics to succeed. Julia shared her adaptation of classic French technique and gave us all the confidence to have fun in the kitchen. Thank you, Julia! The two dishes from MIDA, "Steak and Potatoes" and "MIDA Insalata Supremo" complement each other, bringing balance and exciting technique to a full meal - while offering room for creative interpretation, much like Julia did."

Serves 2.

Ingredients

Prime Rib Eye
1 large boneless rib-eye steak (about 2-2½ lb)
Salt and pepper to taste
About 2 Tbsp basic oil (on reserve) to use as needed (such as canola or vegetable oil)
½ lb butter (about 2 sticks) at room temperature
1 onion, peeled and quartered
4 cloves garlic, peeled

Vegetables
2 russet potatoes, diced into 2 inch pieces
1 bell pepper, diced into 1 inch chunks
¼ cup red wine or balsamic vinegar
1 cup parsley, chopped
Kosher Salt and pepper

Jus
2 cups red wine
1 tsp Dijon or whole grain mustard

Preparation

Start by blanching the potatoes. Using a medium sized pot, place diced potatoes in empty pot. Add two heavy pinches of salt and fill pot with water, 1 inch above potatoes. Turn heat to high and bring to a boil, immediately turn off heat, drain potatoes and set aside.
In a heavy pan or cast iron skillet, heat 2 **tablespoons** of basic oil to about medium/ high heat in preparation for the steak.

Season the steak with salt and pepper. Once the pan and oil are hot, place the steak in pan. After 30 seconds, check the meat for even browning and rotate in pan, ensuring an even sear, repeating for about 2 minutes. Next, flip the steak to the other side and repeat process for another 2 minutes.

Add softened butter, a little at a time to the pan. Then add quartered onion and whole peeled garlic, and begin basting steak for about 4-5 minutes, depending on size. Once the beef has reached desired tenderness, remove steak, onions, and garlic from pan, let rest for about 5 minutes. Reserve excess fat in a side bowl for later use.

Using the same pan, add the blanched potatoes, diced red peppers, and add two tablespoons of fat (from the steak) back to the pan. Sauté on medium high heat for about 6 minutes tossing to evenly cook throughout. Add vinegar, toss until it is soaked up by the potatoes, and season with salt and pepper and set aside.

To make the jus, using the same pan, add red wine and mustard, and place on high heat. Using a wooden spoon, scrape the sides and bottom of the pan, loosening all the flavorful bits of the meat, vegetables, and butter solids. Stir and cook down by ¾ and set aside.

To plate, slice steak and spoon over hot jus, and serve potato, peppers, onions, and garlic on the side.

Roast Rack of Lamb with Semolina and Spinach Gnocchi
Chef Jimmy Burke

Serves 8.

Ingredients for the Lamb
2 whole lamb racks split (4-halves) frenched and trimmed
2 sprigs fresh rosemary
Peel of 1 lemon
4 cloves garlic sliced
1 cup olive oil
Salt and pepper

Ingredients for the Gnocchi
1 quart milk
1 ¼ cup semolina
¾ c. grated Romano or Parmesan cheese
2 egg yolks
8 oz. raw spinach cleaned and blanched
Salt and pepper to taste

Preparation for the Gnocchi (which can be made one day in advance)
Squeeze the excess water from the cooked spinach and puree in a food processor
with the egg yolks. Heat the milk until near boiling, slowly add the semolina and stir
with a wire whip until smooth (the mixture will be thick). Continue stirring with a
wooden spoon over low heat. Add cheese, salt, and pepper, and the egg spinach
mixture. Stir well for one minute then remove from heat. Using a slightly greased
cookie sheet pan, pour the gnocchi mixture into the pan and spread evenly. Let cool.
When mixture has cooled down cut into any shape you desire, round, triangle,
square, etc. and place in a lightly greased baking pan.

Preparation for the Lamb
Combine the oil, rosemary, lemon peel, garlic, and pepper. Mix and coat the lamb
racks, let marinate one day. Preheat oven to 400. Wrap the lamb bones with foil to
protect them during cooking. Season the lamb with salt. Sear the lamb over high
heat either over a grill or in a sauté pan. Place in a roasting pan and cook in a 400
degree oven for 10-15 minutes, let rest for 10 minutes before cutting. In the
meantime, put the gnocchi in the same 400 degree oven and heat through. Place 1 or
2 gnocchi on each plate and cut the lamb racks into 4 chops per plate. Serve with a
rich red wine reduction sauce using either lamb or veal flavored stock with
rosemary. Garnish with roasted plum tomatoes and a sprig of rosemary.

Skillet Cooked Hanger Steak
with Blue Cheese Butter
Chef Gordon Hamersley

Serves 4.

Ingredients

1 shallot, minced
2 Tbsp butter
2 Tbsp blue cheese
2 tsp chopped parsley
4-6 Tbsp cooking oil
2 hanger steaks, 6-8 ounces each, trimmed of the tough tendon and fat by the butcher
Salt & pepper

Preparation

In a small bowl mash together the shallots, butter, blue cheese and parsley.
Keep refrigerated until ready to use.

Heat 3-4 tablespoons of cooking oil in large heavy sauté pans or cast iron skillets until very hot. Season the steaks with salt and pepper, add the steaks to the pan, and reduce the heat to medium high. Cook for 3 minutes on each side, depending on how thick the steaks are.

Place the steaks on warm plates with the blue cheese butter melting on top.
Serve with mashed potato cakes and a simple green salad.

Gratin of Mussels, Country Ham, and Potatoes
Chef Gordon Hamersley

Serves 6.

Ingredients

40-50 mussels
1 ½ cups white wine
1 pinch fresh thyme
1 pinch red pepper flakes
1 pinch fennel seeds
½ white onion, peeled and thinly sliced
1 Tbsp butter
1 Tbsp flour
1 ½ cups heavy cream
1 Tbsp olive oil
4 cups spinach, washed but not dried
8 oz country ham, cut into ½ inch dice
1 russet potato, peeled and cut into very thin rounds
1 ½ cup coarse fresh bread crumbs
2 tsp olive oil
Salt and pepper

Preparation

Pre-heat oven to 350 degrees.
Preparation: Wash the mussels in cold water and remove the beards. Combine the mussels, white wine, thyme, and red pepper flakes, fennel seeds, and onion in a saucepan. Cover and bring the mussels to a boil. When the mussels open they are done. Lift the mussels and onions out of the liquid with a slotted spoon and allow to cool. Remove the mussels from shells and reserve. Strain the liquid. There should be 2 cups of liquid.

Reduce the mussel liquid over moderate heat by half or until 1 cup remains. Add the cream and reduce over low heat to 2 cups. Reserve.

Make a roux in a sauce pan. Melt the butter until it bubbles and add the flour. Cook over low heat for 3-4 minutes stirring. Slowly whisk the mussel cream into the roux until well combined. Cook over low heat for 5 minutes. Approximately 2 cups should remain.

In a sauté pan heat 1 tablespoon olive oil until moderately hot. Add the spinach and season with salt. Cook until the spinach is wilted. Strain and press the excess water out of the spinach, reserve.

Combine the spinach, mussels, onion, and ham in a bowl. Line the bottom of a gratin dish 10 inches round and 1½ inches deep with a single layer of potato. Place half of the mussel mixture on top of the potato in an even layer. Place another layer of potato slices on top of the mussels. Place the remaining mussel mixture on top of the potatoes.

Using a large spoon or medium ladle, pour the mussel cream sauce over the surface of the gratin. Press down slightly on the gratin to evenly distribute the sauce. Sprinkle with salt and pepper to taste.

Cover the gratin dish with aluminum foil and place on a small pan. Bake in a 350 degree oven for 45 minutes.

The potatoes should be tender. Remove the cover and sprinkle on a thin coating of bread crumbs, and drizzle with the olive oil. Return to the oven uncovered for an additional 10 minutes or until the crumbs are browned.

Allow the gratin to rest and cool for a few minutes before serving. Using a serving spoon, scoop out the gratin onto plates. Serve with crusty bread and seasonal salad.

Yankee Pot Roast
Chef Peter Davis

Ingredients

1- 4 lb piece of chuck
4 Tbsp oil
3 cloves garlic
2 carrots roughly chopped
3 celery sticks roughly chopped
1 medium onion roughly chopped
3 cups veal stock
1 cup red wine
2 bay leaves
2 sprigs fresh thyme
4 carrot cut batonnets
4 parsnips cut batonnets
4 Tbsp chopped parsley

Preparation

Preheat the oven to 350 degrees. Place a heavy bottomed pot on the stove over medium heat. Add the oil to the pot and when it is hot, add the chuck (fat side down). Cook the fat side until brown, then brown all sides of the meat, and remove from the pot. Place the rough chopped onion, celery, carrot, and garlic into the pot until well browned. Add the red wine to the pot, reduce by one half. Put the meat, veal stock, bay leaf, and thyme in the pot, bring to a boil and place the pot in the oven uncovered.
Cook the pot roast 2½ hours, turning every half hour. If the sauce reduces too much, add 1 cup of water.

While the pot roast is cooking, roast the carrot and parsnip batonnets in the 350 degree oven for 30 minutes. Cool and place aside.

Remove the pot roast from the oven and take out the meat. Remove excess fat from the sauce. Puree the sauce and season with salt and pepper.

Slice the meat in ½ inch slices and arrange on a platter. Pour the sauce over the meat and garnish with the reheated carrot and parsnip. Sprinkle with chopped celery.

Beet Risotto with Arugula & Carpaccio of Beef
Chef Daniele Baliani

Serves 6.

Ingredients for Risotto

2 Tbsp extra virgin olive oil
1 medium sized onion, finely chopped
1 ½ cups Arborio or Carnaroli rice
2 tsp salt
1 cup dry white wine
5 cups homemade chicken broth
2 medium sized beets, boiled until tender and pureed in food processor.

To Finish

1 Tbsp butter
3 Tbsp Parmesan "Reggiano" cheese
Salt and Pepper to taste

For Garnish

2 bunches of arugula, washed and dressed with oil & vinegar
6 very thin slices of beef sirloin
2 Tbsp truffle oil (optional)
Parmesan shavings

Preparation

Place 2 tablespoons of olive oil in 2 quart casserole over medium flame. Add the chopped onion and sweat until translucent. Add the rice and slowly toast without browning until the rice begins to "pop." Deglaze with the white wine and reduce until dry. Add enough chicken stock to cover the rice. Simmer slowly, and continue adding stock as the rice absorbs the liquid until completely cooked (approximately 18-20 min.) Finish by adding 2 tablespoons of beet puree. Off the flame, fold in the remaining butter and Parmesan cheese.

Presentation

Spoon the beet risotto on a medium size plate. Garnish with the dressed arugula salad and one slice of the beef sirloin wrapped around the risotto. Finish with a drizzle of the truffle oil and the Parmesan shavings.

BUON APPETITO!!!

Lamb Shank Tagine with Prunes and Apricots
Chef Alia Meddeb

Ingredients

Lamb shank
½ onion ground in Cuisinart
½ Tbsp ginger
¼ Tbsp turmeric
1 tsp black pepper
5 Tbsp olive oil

Preparation

Mix onions and seasonings together with the olive oil. Put in a clay pot (tagine), add the lamb shank, and cover tightly. Bake for 3 hours at 375 degrees. Turn the lamb shank every 30 minutes and add a little water (¼ cup) with each turn as needed.

Make Syrup
2 cups honey
1 Tbsp cinnamon
½ tsp saffron
½ tsp ginger
1 cup dried prunes
1 cup dried apricots

Bring to a boil, then add the prunes and apricots, cook for 5 minutes then shut it off. Let cool.

For Serving
When lamb shank is cooked off the bone, add the prune and apricot syrup. Garnish with toasted almonds and sesame seeds and add a drop of orange blossom. Serve with steamed couscous.

Leapin' John
Chef Kevin Conner

Rice and Peas with Sausage and Seared Duck is a newer take on the traditional southern dish Hoppin' John

Ingredients for the Rice and Peas

¾ cup diced Andouille sausage
4 Tbsp chopped garlic
1 small yellow onion
1 stalk of celery
1 green pepper
7 oz dry black-eyed peas or field peas
1 tsp paprika
2 tsp garlic powder
2 tsp kosher salt
8 sprigs of thyme
2 bay leaves
3 cups chicken stock
Rice

Preparation for the Rice and Peas

Pre-soak peas overnight or at least for 4 hours to shorten the cooking time. Next cut the Andouille sausage into small pieces and cook it slowly in a medium pot over medium-low heat. Once the sausage is crispy, increase the heat to medium-high and add the celery, onion, green pepper, and garlic, and sauté until they begin to get soft, about 3-4 minutes. When the garlic begins to brown, add your seasoning and stir for one minute. Then begin to add the black-eyed peas, bay leaf, thyme, 3 cups of chicken stock and bring to a simmer. Cook for an hour or until the peas are tender (not mushy). While the black-eyed peas are cooking, cook the rice separately according to package instructions. When the peas and rice are done, gently mix well to incorporate together.

Ingredients for the Duck

Braised duck legs
2 duck legs
2 tsp kosher salt
1 tsp black pepper
1 Tbsp olive oil

Preparation for the Duck

Pre-heat oven to 325 degrees. Generously season both sides of the duck legs and heat a sauté pan to medium-high heat. (Make sure that the pan can fit both duck legs). Add oil to the pan and begin to sear the duck legs, skin side down first, for 4 minutes on each side. After the duck legs are seared on each side add flavorful chicken stock to the pan, make sure there's enough chicken stock to cover the duck legs. Allow the stock to get to a rolling simmer. Cover the pan with a lid or foil and braise in the oven until fork tender (1 hour). Allow to cool and pick the meat off the bone, then add to the peas, sausage, and rice.

Seared Duck Breast Topping

1 or 2 duck breast
Salt and pepper to taste

Using a sharp knife, score the breast in a cross-hatch pattern along the skin about a ¼ inch apart. Do not score to the flesh of the duck, just to the point where you can see the score marks. Remove any excess skin along the side of the duck breast. Place duck breasts, skin side down, in a large, cold sauté pan. Do not add any oil to the pan, the fat from the skin will begin to melt from the duck breast. Place pan over low to medium-low heat. To keep the edges from curling up, press duck breasts down with spatula. Every two minutes, as the fat begins to accumulate, drain the pan of the excess fat and return the pan to the heat. Continue to do this process until much of the fat has rendered and skin is golden brown. This typically takes about 8-10 minutes. Increase heat to medium and flip the meat to the flesh side and begin cooking on this side. For medium-rare meat, cook until breast registers 130 degrees about 1 to 2 minutes. Continue cooking until duck registers 140 degrees F for medium or 155 degrees F for well-done. Remove duck from pan and set aside to rest.

Presentation

Top the rice and peas with slices of the duck breast and serve.

Desserts

Raspberry Almond Bars
Chefs Ihsan and Valerie Gurdal

Ingredients

Crust
1 cup all-purpose flour
¼ cup granulated sugar
¼ tsp salt
1 stick (4 oz.) unsalted butter, cold
½ cup American Spoon Raspberry Preserves**
Preheat oven 350 degrees

Filling
2 large eggs
1 cup brown sugar
1 tsp Nielsen-Massey vanilla extract
2 tsp salt
⅛ tsp baking soda

Preparation

For the Crust
Mix flour, sugar, and salt in mixer bowl with paddle attachment. Cut cold butter into small pieces and mix flour until in resembles cornmeal. Press into buttered and floured 8 inch square pan. Bake in preheated oven for 18-20 minutes or until pastry is light brown. Spread immediately with Â½ cup American Spoon Raspberry preserves. Set aside while you make filling.

For the Filling
Combine all ingredients in a mixer bowl with paddle attachment and mix for about 1 minute on medium speed, until well combined. Pour over crust. Sprinkle 1 cup sliced almonds evenly over top. Bake for 20-22 minutes until top is golden brown and does not jiggle when lightly shaken. Cool on rack and cut into 16 small squares.

Topping
1 cup sliced almonds**

**You may substitute any of your favorite preserves or nuts to make this versatile bar recipe.

Lemon Cornmeal Cookies
Chefs Ihsan and Valerie Gurdal

Ingredients

1 stick butter or ½ cup, softened
¾ cup brown sugar
1 egg
1 tsp vanilla extract
Zest of one lemon
1 ¾ cup all-purpose flour
½ cup cornmeal
1 tsp baking powder
½ tsp baking soda
½ tsp salt
½ cup sour cream

Preparation

Cream butter and brown sugar until light and fluffy, about 3 minutes. Add egg, vanilla extract, and lemon zest. Mix until combined, about 1 minute. Sift together dry ingredients. Add to butter mixture with sour cream. Mix just until combined, 30 seconds to 1 minute.

Use teaspoon to scoop onto lightly greased cookie sheets. Bake at 350 degrees for approximately 15 minutes or until light brown and top springs back when lightly pressed. Cool on racks and store airtight.

Makes approximately 36 cookies.

Maple Crème Brulee
Chef Lydia Shire

Ingredients

1 quart heavy cream
1 ¼ cups maple syrup
9 egg yolks
Pinch salt

Preparation

Heat cream until hot.
In a bowl, mix yolks and maple syrup together, stirring well.
Slowly add hot cream to above mixture.
Strain through fine sieve if lumpy.
Add pinch of salt.
Pour into crusted cups.
Bake in hot water-bath 300 degrees about 40 minutes.
Cool and chill in refrigerator. Ideally, make mixture a day ahead and let stand to avoid bubbles on surface.
When ready to serve, sprinkle granulated sugar on top, and caramelize under broiler (sugar should melt and turn brown).

Sweet Potato – Chocolate Nut Cake
Chef Marian Morash

The natural sweet potato orange color looks beautiful swirled together with chocolate, while the flavors complement each other. Sprinkle this cake with confectioner's sugar or drizzle it with the sugar glaze that follows recipe.

Ingredients

4 oz semi sweet chocolate
1 tsp vanilla extract
3 cups flour
1 ½ cups sugar
2 tsp baking powder
2 tsp baking soda
2 tsp cinnamon
½ tsp ground ginger

¼ tsp ground cloves
¼ tsp nutmeg
1 tsp salt
2 cups mashed cooked sweet potatoes
1 ½ cups vegetable oil
4 eggs
1 cup chopped nuts

Preparation

Butter and lightly flour a 10-inch tube pan. Place chocolate and vanilla in a small saucepan, and set, covered, in a larger pan that you've just filled with boiling water.

Sift together all dry ingredients and set aside. In a large bowl, beat the sweet potatoes and oil together, then beat in the eggs one by one until well blended. Slowly add dry ingredients and mix well, stir in nuts. Put one-third of the mixture in another bowl and stir in the chocolate, which should be melted smooth by now. Alternate the batters in a tube pan, as you would with a marble cake. With a knife, cut through the two batters to slightly swirl together. Bake in a preheated 350 degree oven for 1 – 1¼ hours or until the sides have shrunk away from the pan, the top is springy, and tester comes out dry. Let cool 10 minutes and then remove from the pan and cool on a rack. (Makes a 10 inch tube cake)

Sugar Glaze:

2-3 Tbsp boiling water
1 ½ cups confectioners' sugar

Beat water gradually into sugar until mixture has the consistency of a thick cream sauce, drizzle over cake

Lemon Ice
Chef Deborah Hughes and Mary-Catherine Deibel

Ingredients

2 cups fresh lemon juice
2 cups fresh orange juice
2 cups sugar
2 cups heavy cream

Preparation

Mix all the ingredients together. Freeze in metal container. When frozen, whip in standing mixer. Add more lemon juice and orange juice for flavor, as desired. Add more cream if desired.

Apple Charlotte with Apricot – Caran

Chef Deborah Hughes and Mary-Cathe

Ingredients

6 lb Granny Smith apples (about 4 quarts)
1½ cup apricot preserves
1 cup granulated sugar
1 Tbsp vanilla
½ cup dark rum
5 Tbsp. butter
½ cup Grand Marnier
¼ cup Calvados

Preparation

Peel, core and quarter all the apples. Slice into ⅛ inch pieces. Place in heavy bottom pan, cover, and cook over low heat for about 40 minutes, stirring occasionally until the apples have lost most of their moisture and form very thick paste, thick enough to coat a wooden spoon.

Force preserves through a sieve, then reserve ½ cup of the strained preserves. Mix the other half with the rest of the above ingredients. Add this mixture to apple paste. Cook the apple-apricot paste over medium heat, stirring constantly to bring the mixture back to a thick paste.

Heat oven to 425 degrees

12 slices brioche bread, cut into 4 inch squares, each a ¼ inch thick
1 cup clarified butter
6-cup 4-inch-high charlotte mold

Remove crusts. Cut 4 semi-circles and one square large enough to cover the bottom of the mold. Slice the rest of the mold with the sautéed bread sitting the slices tightly together. Reserve eight bread strips to form a top for the charlotte. See below for baking and assembling instructions.

Caramel Sauce

sugar
cup water
2 Tbsp rum
1 Tbsp Grand Marnier
2 Tbsp Calvados
2 Tbsp butter

Place sugar and water in a sauce pan and bring to a boil. Do not stir, but brush down sides of pot with a pastry brush dipped into water every two minutes or so (to prevent the formulation of a grainy caramel). When the sugar turns a golden brown caramel color, add the remaining ½ cup of strained apricot preserves and the rest of the ingredients. Stir over medium heat until thick.

To Assemble Apple Charlotte with Apricot Caramel Sauce

Pour the apple paste into the breaded mold, forming a dome at the top. Cover the domed apple mixture with the remaining 8 stripes of bread. Bake the charlotte for 30 minutes at 425 degrees until the top is brown. After baking and cooling, the dome will sink so that it forms a flat bottom for unmolding. Pour the apricot caramel sauce over the top of the whole charlotte just before serving.

Country Apple Tart
Chef Jacques Pepin

This tart – possibly the most "French" of all desserts – is one I make often at home and especially like for buffet-style entertaining. Guests pick up pieces as they would slices of pizza and eat them lukewarm or at room temperature. It is difficult to make for four so I have enough here for eight. Any leftovers will disappear quickly enough!

The dough, made with only a cup of flour, should be rolled to a very thin rectangle. Although the tart can be made in a conventional pie mold or tart ring, I do it free-form instead, so that no trimming is necessary and all the dough is used. Be sure to cook the tart for a long time – at least an hour; the pastry should be dark brown and crusty and the apples tender. It is important to use only the amount of apples called for in this recipe. People tend to use more, thinking it will make the tart even better, but a thin layer of apples is more effective for this tart. The finished tart has a wonderfully rustic, "country" look. Serves 8.

Ingredients

Tart Dough
1 cup all-purpose flour (about 5 ounces)
1 Tbsp sugar
2½ ounces (⅔ stick) cold unsalted butter, cut into ½ inch pieces
2½ Tbsp ice water

Apple Topping
4 Golden Delicious apples (1¾ lb total)
1 Tbsp honey
2 Tbsp sugar
½ tsp ground cinnamon
1 Tbsp unsalted butter

Preparation

Place the flour, sugar, and butter for the tart dough in the bowl of a food processor, and process the mixture for about 5 seconds. Add the water, and process for about 10 seconds, or until the dough just begins to come together. There should still be pieces of butter visible in the dough. Refrigerate the dough while you prepare the apples.

Preheat oven to 400 degrees.

Peel, halve, and core the apples. Arrange them, cut side down, on a cutting board, and cut them crosswise into ¼ inch slices. Set aside the larger center slices, and chop the end slices and any broken slices coarsely (about half the slices should be sliced, half chopped).

On a lightly flowered work surface, roll the dough to create a 12-by-14-inch rectangle. Transfer the rectangle to a cookie sheet.

Arrange the chopped apples on the dough, spreading them out within 1 inch of the edge. Sprinkle the honey over the chopped apples. Arrange the apple slices in one layer on top of the chopped apples, positioning them in slightly overlapping rows, so that the rounded edge of one slice is visible behind the following slice.

In a small bowl, mix together the topping, sugar and cinnamon. Sprinkle this mixture on top of the sliced apples, and dot them with the 1 tbsp butter.

Fold the edge of the pastry over the apples to create a 1-inch border. Bake the tart for 60 minutes, or until the pastry is brown and crisp, and the apples tender. Cut the tart into eight pieces. Serve it lukewarm or room temperature.

Chocolate Bread Pudding
Chef Roger Berkowitz and Richard Vellante

Serves 18 (Lasagna pan).

Ingredients:

2 lb dark chocolate	1 lb butter
18 eggs	2 quarts heavy cream
3½ cups sugar	1½ tsp vanilla extract
1 loaf white bread	1 tsp cinnamon

Preparation

Chop chocolate and place into a stainless mixing bowl with butter.
Break eggs, and mix with 1¾ cups sugar.

Cut the crust off the bread, dice into 1 inch cubes and place in lasagna pan.
Fill a pot halfway with water. Bring it to a boil and place bowl with chocolate and butter over the boiling water. Stir until melted together thoroughly. The mixture should look smooth.

Place cream, vanilla, 1¾ cups sugar, and cinnamon into another pot, and carefully bring to a boil. The sugar will protect the cream from scorching, and will not burn, so don't stir until you see some steam rising from the top. Watch carefully, when cream comes to a boil, it will foam and rise quickly and you will spend an eternity cleaning up.

When chocolate and butter mixture is melted together properly, you will need to temper the egg mixture. Do this SLOWLY, whisking in small amount of chocolate mixture into egg mixture until all the chocolate has been added to the eggs.

Pour the chocolate/egg mixture over bread cubes and mix with your hands.
Put into the refrigerator and allow the bread to soak up the chocolate/egg mixture.
Allow at least 2 hours; it is best if left overnight.

Bake in a 350 degree oven until completely set. This dessert holds very well.
You can cut it into portions after it has cooled, wrap them in plastic wrap, pull them out one at a time, and microwave them to reheat.

Souffléd Lemon Custard
Chef Gordon Hamersley

Ingredients

½ cup butter
1½ cups sugar
6 eggs, separated
1 cup lemon juice
⅔ cup flour, sifted
¼ tsp lemon zest, chopped
2 cups milk
1 cup cream
1 pinch salt

Preparation

In a KitchenAid, with the paddle attachment, cream the butter and sugar together until fluffy.

Add the egg yolks one at a time. Add the lemon juice, flour, and lemon zest until just barely combined. Remove to a large bowl.

Stir in the milk and cream until smooth but do not over mix.

In a separate bowl, beat the egg whites until they hold soft-medium peaks, adding a pinch of salt halfway through. Fold into the custard mixture. Pour the custard mixture into a 9x11x2 inch pan. Bake at 350 degrees in a bain-marie for about 50 minutes or until the custard is just set. Let cool to room temperature and serve.

Chocolate Espresso Torte
Chef Gordon Hamersley

Ingredients

¾ lb unsalted butter
½ cup white sugar
½ cup dark brown sugar
12 ounces semi-sweet chocolate, chopped
1 Tbsp instant espresso coffee
1 cup strong brewed espresso coffee
6 eggs
6 egg yolks

Preparation

Heat the oven to 350 degrees. Line the bottom of a 9-inch cake pan with parchment and lightly butter the bottom and sides of the pan.

Melt the butter, sugars, chocolate, instant espresso, and brewed espresso in a saucepan slowly until the chocolate and sugars are soft. Whisk to combine. Do not boil. Place the eggs and egg yolks into a medium bowl and lightly whisk to just combine.

Add the eggs to the chocolate mixture and lightly whisk to combine.

Pour the batter into the cake pan and place the cake pan into a larger 12-inch round sauté pan with sides at least 2 inches high. Fill the larger pan with water so that it rides halfway up the side of the cake pan.

Place the pans into the oven and bake for about 45 minutes to one hour. The torte is cooked when a skewer placed in the center of the torte comes away clean.

Carefully remove the torte from the pan with the water and place on a wire rack to cool. About 1 hour. Then refrigerate overnight to cool completely.

When ready to serve, place the torte pan on a low flame stove burner for about 8-10 seconds. This will help release the torte from the pan. Invert the torte onto a plate and re-invert it, top-side up, onto a serving platter.

Cut with a warm, dry knife on to plates and serve with whipped cream, ice cream or crème anglaise.

Polenta Pound Cake
Chef Daniele Baliani

Ingredients

8 oz butter, soft
1 tsp lemon zest, finely chopped
2 cups sugar
6 eggs separated
1 tsp vanilla
½ tsp baking soda
1 cup sour cream
1¼ cup cornmeal
2 cups flour
½ tsp salt

Preparation

Heat oven 325 degrees. Butter 9" loaf pan and dust with cornmeal (¼ cup).
Beat butter and lemon zest till light and fluffy, slowly adding 1 ½ cups of sugar.
Beat in yolks one at a time. Add vanilla, baking soda, and sour cream. Mix well.
Add 1 cup cornmeal, flour, and salt. In separate bowl, whip whites until stiff,
slowly adding remaining ½ cup sugar. Fold into batter. Bake at 325 degrees for an
hour to an hour and a half.

Lemon Mousse
Chef Andrée Robert

This was a favorite at Maison Robert. It is light as a cloud and yet it is bursting with flavor. Serves 10 to 15.

Ingredients

5 large egg yolks
½ cup sugar
1 Tbsp gelatin
Zest and juice from 2 lemons
Zest and juice from 1 orange
5 large egg whites
½ cup sugar
1⅔ cup heavy cream

Preparation

In a double boiler with the water just barely simmering put the yolks and ½ cup sugar. (I prefer to use a stainless steel bowl on top of a pan of water because there are no corners in the bowl.) Make sure that the water does not touch the top pan. Beat the yolks and sugar on high with an electric beater until a ribbon forms (about 5 minutes) and the mixture is pale yellow. Remove from heat and let cool slightly.

Meanwhile heat lemon and orange juice, and zest and gelatin over low heat, stirring occasionally, until gelatin is melted. Remove from heat and add to yolks. Beat to incorporate and stir occasionally to cool down.

Pour the egg whites and ½ cup sugar in another stainless steel bowl. Put over still warm water in the pan, but do not turn the heat on. Beat with an electric beater until the whites form stiff peaks. Fold the whites into the yolk mixture.

Clean out the bowl from the whites and add the heavy cream. Beat with the electric beater until stiff peaks form. Fold the whipped cream into the yolk mixture. Cover and refrigerate for at least 2 hours, or overnight.

Serve chilled with raspberry coulis, or strawberry compote.

Cranberry-Black Walnut Pound Cake
Chef Jasper White

A pound cake is a dense cake that was originally made with a pound of butter, a pound of sugar, a pound of eggs, a pound of flour, and nothing else. Many different flavors and garnishes can be used, but the key to a good pound cake is butter. Very fresh butter of the highest quality available is called for.

Makes one 9-inch loaf cake.

Ingredients

¾ lb unsalted butter
1 lb confectioners' sugar, sifted
6 whole eggs
1 Tbsp pure vanilla extract
2 cups sifted cake flour
1 Tbsp lemon juice
2 Tbsp grated lemon rind
1 cup black walnut pieces, coarsely chopped
1 cup fresh or frozen cranberries, coarsely chopped
Confectioners' sugar for dusting

Preparation

Preheat oven to 300 degrees. Lightly butter and flour a 9-inch tube pan; set aside.

Cream the butter and sugar in a mixing bowl, beating until light and fluffy. Add the eggs, one at a time, continuing to beat. Add the lemon juice and vanilla. Now gently fold in the flour, followed by the lemon rind, walnuts, and cranberries.

Pour into the prepared cake pan and bake in the preheated oven for about 1 hour 30 minutes. Test by inserting toothpick; it should come out clean.

Cook in the pan on a wire rack for 10 minutes, then unmold, and place on a rack to cool thoroughly. Sprinkle with sifted confectioners' sugar and serve at room temperature.

Strawberry Shortcake
Chef Jasper White

Probably the best loved of all American desserts, shortcake is also one of the simplest - nothing but fresh fruit, whipped cream, and biscuits or cake. Its success depends almost entirely on the quality of the ingredients not on the expertise of the cook. It is the epitome of simple country cooking.

Ideally this dessert is made with berries or other local fruit still warm from the sun, picked that day and never refrigerated. Raspberries, blackberries, peaches, nectarines, and most other fruits and berries can be used as well as strawberries. Fruits should be sliced and berries left whole or sliced only if very large. Sometimes, particularly if I am making a whole cake, I like to macerate the fruit in wine or liqueur for a few minutes before assembling the dessert to extract some of the juice and create a very intensively flavored syrup. If you do this, use the wine or liqueur sparingly so that it does not overpower the fruit. The following recipe is for traditional short cake, the dough can be made into either cake or biscuits. Serves 8.

Ingredients for Shortcake or Biscuits

2 cups sifted all-purpose flour
⅓ cup granulated sugar
4 tsp baking powder
½ tsp salt
8 Tbsp (1 stick) unsalted butter
1 egg, beaten
⅓ cup milk
3 to 4 pints strawberries
Granulated sugar (about 1 cup)
Simple syrup, sherry, port or other sweet wine or Grand Marnier or other fruit based liqueur for macerating (optional)
4 cups sweetened whipped cream
Confectioners' sugar (optional)

Preparation

Preheat the oven to 400 degrees. Generously butter a 7-or 8-inch oven proof skillet or an 8-inch cake pan for a whole cake or a sheet pan for biscuits; set aside.

Sift together the flour, sugar, baking powder, and salt into a mixing bowl. Cut butter into small pieces, about the size of a hazelnut, and add the flour to the mixture; mix gently. Add the egg and milk, and mix just until the dough sticks together; knead gently.

For a cake, transfer the dough to the prepared skillet or cake pan and shape it, patting gently; place in a preheated oven and bake for 20 to 25 minutes or until lightly browned. For biscuits, drop the dough on the sheet pan, bake for 15 to 20 minutes or until lightly browned. Time the baking so that the shortcake or biscuits are still warm when served.

While the shortcake or biscuits are baking, hull the strawberries. Set aside a few of the best ones to put on top. Cut the rest of the berries in half if they are very large. Sprinkle with sugar to taste, and, if desired, a few drops of syrup, sweet wine or liqueur; set aside. Whip the cream and put it in the refrigerator until ready to assemble cake.

Split the shortcake or biscuits while warm. If you are serving a whole cake, cover the bottom half with berries, preferably macerated, and put a bit of whipped cream on top. Cover with the other layer and top with the rest of whipped cream. Decorate with the strawberries that were set aside and serve immediately.
If you are using biscuits, put a large dollop of whipped cream on the bottom half of each biscuit (some will run out) and top with fruit. Cover with top half. Decorate with the strawberries that were set aside. Dust with sifted confectioners' sugar.

Ingredients for Sweetened Whipped Cream

Thick farm-fresh cream, not homogenized, is best for whipping. It should be only very lightly flavored with vanilla and sweetened with a little sugar. If farm-fresh cream is not available, buy heavy or extra-heavy cream, not so-called whipping cream, which has the bare minimum of butterfat needed.

Makes two cups
1 cup heavy cream
½ tsp pure vanilla extract
1 Tbsp granulated sugar

Combine the cream and vanilla in a chilled bowl. Beat until the cream begins to thicken.

Add the sugar and continue beating until the desired consistency is reached. I like soft whipped cream for most uses.

Mignardise

A Musical Confection
Arts & Entertainment Critic Joyce Kulhawik

Over the years, I interviewed my Cambridge neighbor Julia Child many times on TV. When invited to contribute to Julia's farewell gala in 2001, I did what any self-respecting Arts & Entertainment reporter would do. I hired a piano player, created some lyrics, half-baked them into Cole Porter's classic "You're the top!" and sang this "musical confection" to a bemused audience. I will never forget Julia's reaction after my performance, exclaiming in that flutey voice, "Joyce, you're a lot of fun!"

"Julia, You're the Top!"

You're the top!
You're a hot soufflé.
You're the top!
You're crème brulee.
You wrote the book to help us cook Francais
Your Soupe L'oignon,
Your Bourguignon,
Are just parfait!
You're foie gras,
You're a pile of truffles,
No faux pas ever ruffles.
We're flat champagne that tries in vain to pop,

But if, Julia, we're the bottom you're the top!

You're the top!
You're savoir faire.
You're the top!
You're sole meuniere.
You're the cake that rises and no surprise it's delish!
You're a fresh baguette.
You're crepe suzette,
You're quite a dish!
You're magnifique
You're like Versailles
My critique?
You're nonpareil.
We're a lumpy mousse and our goose is cooked and a flop

But if, Julia, we're the bottom you're the top!

Arts & Entertainment Critic
Joyce Kulhawik

Joyce Kulhawik, best known as the Emmy Award-winning Arts & Entertainment critic for WBZ-TV (CBS-Boston) has covered local and national events from Boston and Broadway to Hollywood. Born into a food-centric Polish/Italian family, with a huge appetite, Joyce has been known to consume three times her weight in pasta. She loves to bake, hates to cook, but ever the critic, cannot resist analyzing the recipes she will never execute to figure out what makes them tick--much the way she approaches movies and theater. She is currently President of the Boston Theater Critics Association and a member of the Boston Society of Film Critics. She has co-hosted nationally-syndicated movie-review shows with Roger Ebert and Leonard Maltin. Find her reviews at JoycesChoices.com.

Joyce is also a 3-time cancer survivor and addressed Congress on the 20th anniversary of the National Cancer Act. She has been a very public advocate in the fight against the disease, including emceeing the annual Hoffman Breast Center fundraiser for the last 20 years. Among countless awards for her career and advocacy, Kulhawik has received the N.E.Emmy's Governor's Award for her distinguished career, was an inaugural inductee into the Massachusetts Broadcasters Hall of Fame, has an endowed scholarship in her name at the Berklee College of Music and received the American Cancer Society's National Bronze Medal. She also holds an Honorary Doctorate in Communications from her alma mater Simmons University, and hosts the annual Simmons Leadership Conference here and abroad,the longest-running conference for professional women in the world.

About the Chefs

Chef Jody Adams

In 2016, James Beard Award-winning Chef Jody Adams shut the doors on her Harvard Square restaurant Rialto after an extraordinary 22-year run. Great food, in her view, no longer depended on a fine dining environment. She turned her attention to the Boston restaurants she built and runs with partners Eric Papachristos, Sean Griffing and Jon Mendez. The lively restaurant TRADE had been rocking on the Greenway in the financial district since 2011. Saloniki, a fast-casual Greek restaurant in the Fenway, has had lines snaking out the door from its opening day in 2016; its Kendall Square spinoff, opened later that year, is equally popular. A third Saloniki opened in Harvard Square in October 2018. Finally, diners looking for a taste of Adams' signature Mediterranean dishes without the white-tablecloth formality have found a safe harbor in Porto, a full-service restaurant next to Sak's Fifth Avenue that opened a few months before Rialto closed. "I never stand still," Adams says. With a closetful of "best" awards for her food and restaurants, Adams is proudest of her work advocating for children's welfare or combating hunger through her support of the Boston Food Bank. In 2010 she received the Humanitarian of the Year Award from Share Our Strength. During regular visits to Haiti, she has helped to shape the hospitality programs for Partners In Health facilities. Adams might now be perched at the pinnacle of her career, except that another pinnacle might be just around the corner. In late September a TRADE opened at Terminal B at Logan airport and in early October of this year, Greek Street, a spinoff of Saloniki opened in TimeOut Boston Market. She's definitely not standing still. In 2018 Chef Adams was inducted into The James Beard Foundation Who's Who of Food & Beverage in America. (*photo by Ken Rivard*)

Chef Daniele Baliani

As a scholar-athlete at Columbia University in the mid 1980's, Daniele Baliani left soccer and the classroom to reconnect with his Roman roots and pursue a career in cooking. Though a complete novice at the time, Baliani marched into the kitchen of the world famous Le Cirque restaurant in Manhattan and persuaded (a then-unknown) Daniel Boulud to take him under his wing. While finishing his degree, Baliani began an old-world apprenticeship with Chef Boulud who subsequently shipped him off to Europe to further his culinary education in the kitchens of true masters: Alain Ducasse at the Hotel de Paris in Monte Carlo and Pierre Herme' at the famed Patisserie Fauchon in Paris. Following that year in France, he moved back to the land of his upbringing and worked in Michelin star restaurants in Tuscany and Liguria in what can only be described as a living fairytale. He was all of 23 years old. By the mid-90s, Baliani had moved to Boston and made a name for himself first as chef de cuisine at the acclaimed Back Bay restaurant Pignoli, which received three and a half stars from the Boston Globe, and from 2009-12 as Chef de Cuisine at Belmont's Il Casale, which was named one of New England's Best Italian restaurants by Boston Magazine. As befitting his eclectic background, Baliani has created several niches for himself within the industry. He has been a consulting chef to Fortune 500 brands including Barilla, Nestle' and Freschetta Pizza. He was the founder and operator of a meal-delivery service in Manhattan called My Befana and since 2001 he has played the role of educator and businessman as sole proprietor of a boutique travel company Pantheon Adventures, which specializes in gastronomic and cultural tours of the Mediterranean basin. This year Daniele celebrates 30 years of industry experience with an inexhaustible desire to make food that stirs hearts and palates wherever he cooks! (*photo by Claudia Sutherland*)

Chef Roger Berkowitz

Roger started working in the family fish market in Inman Square, Cambridge at the age of 10 and held a variety of roles prior to becoming President and CEO of Legal Sea Foods in 1992. Since taking the helm, he's led the company's growth and diversification. He now oversees restaurant, retail and mail order divisions and steers the course for 4,000 employees. Roger is currently a member of NOAA's Marine Fisheries Advisory Committee and the Regional Selection Panel for the President's Commission on White House Fellowships. He was a member of the Board of Directors for the Federal Reserve Bank of Boston and the Massachusetts Workforce Training Fund Advisory Committee. He is also a member and past President of the Massachusetts Restaurant Association. In addition, Roger serves on many non-profit Boards including: Dana-Farber Cancer Institute, UNICEF and the Environmental League of Massachusetts. He also serves on the leadership council at the Harvard School of Public Health. Roger graduated from the Newhouse School at Syracuse University and attended executive education programs at Harvard Business School, University of London School of Business and Stanford Graduate School of Business. He holds an honorary master's degree from the Culinary Institute of America and honorary doctorates from Johnson & Wales University, Newbury College, Salem State University, Nichols College and New England College of Business. Among numerous awards and recognitions, Roger was named a James Beard Award winner in 2017, received the "Chairman's Award for Distinguished Meritorious Service" from the Atlantic States Marine Fisheries Commission and was inducted into the "Menu Masters Hall of Fame" by Nation's Restaurant News. He was also the recipient of the George Arents Award, which recognizes Syracuse University alumni for their achievements. Roger is the co-host of "Name Brands," a podcast series with CBS Boston and he co-wrote *The New Legal Sea Foods Cookbook.* He was featured in the books *"Dare to Lead! Uncommon Sense and Unconventional Wisdom from 50 Top CEOs"* by Mike Merrill and *"Leadership Secrets of the World's Most Successful CEOs"* by Eric Yaverbaum. (*photo courtesy of Legal Sea Foods*)

Chef Eric Brennan

Eric has always had a deep appreciation for evoking the purest flavors from fresh, local ingredients. After graduating from the Culinary Institute of America in Hyde Park, New York in 1982, Eric worked several years in both New York and The Hamptons on eastern Long Island before landing in Boston as Chef de Cuisine of Aujourd'hui at the Four Seasons Hotel. This started his 12-year career with the luxury hotel and resort group, during which he served as Executive Chef at the Four Seasons Biltmore in Santa Barbara, as well as the Toronto flagship property where he ran the hotel's three restaurants in addition to private dining and room service. In 2000, Eric returned to New England to work for Kenneth Himmel's restaurant company for the next 16 years. He was able to exercise his creativity through seasonally inspired dishes as Executive Chef of Harvest and Excelsior restaurants. From there, he opened Post 390 spearheading a team that helped bring a contemporary touch to the traditional tavern dining experience. Recognized for its 'Farm to Post' tasting series which Eric launched in 2012, he continued to help the restaurant highlight the region's finest farmers, foragers and fishermen through personal relationships, farm selection and visits, and menu development. Eric became the Culinary Director of Himmel Hospitality Group in Boston, overseeing menu development, planning, sourcing and event coordinating for its three restaurants: Grill 23 & Bar, one of Boston's top steakhouse and seafood grills; Post 390, an urban tavern in Back Bay; and Harvest, a culinary institution in Cambridge. After 40 years of dedication, Eric decided to leave restaurants and is now in charge of Fidelity Investments Executive Dining. Eric lives with his wife Lauren in Milton Massachusetts. Their two daughters Jessica and Samantha are both recent college graduates. When not working, Eric enjoys hiking, motorcycling, fishing and gardening. (*photo used by permission of Eric Brennan*)

Chef Jimmy Burke

Jimmy Burke's love affair with food dates back to his childhood, when his parents owned a restaurant in South Boston and he worked there on Saturdays and holidays. At home, food was every bit as important and he was fortunate to have his mother and aunts, all phenomenal cooks, as mentors. "I was always around food and food became part of me," recalls Burke. After high school, he was offered a job on the Cape as a dishwasher and quickly discovered he really enjoyed cooking and loved the energy of the kitchen, so he applied and was accepted to the Culinary Institute of America. After he graduated, he worked under Andreas Meyer, who eventually helped Jimmy land a chef job at Harvest in Cambridge. It was the late '70s and the beginning of celebrity chefs and a three-year period that would prove very influential in his career. Almost immediately, the owners sent Jimmy on a trip to France to inform his palate. He spent three weeks eating at L'Auberge de I'Ill and several other Michelin-rated restaurants and it opened his senses to the complexities and subtleties of French cooking. Back in Cambridge, he became very good friends with Julia Child and often appeared on television with her. He also studied food in Italy at a time when he was trying to formulate in his mind what the French were doing versus what the Italians were doing. They both had a huge influence on his cooking, but the simplicity of Italian cooking won out. After three years at Harvest, Jimmy realized he was ready to be his own boss. There was a restaurant called Allegro for sale in Waltham, Massachusetts, and he bought it. When it opened in 1981, Allegro established a new gold standard in the Boston area that was met for the next ten years. The Tuscan Grille was another ten year run. In 2016, he opened Vivo, a country-style Italian restaurant considered to be one of the best restaurants in the lakes region of Maine. In all, Jimmy has owned and operated twelve restaurants, the last three of which he has co-owned with his wife, Joanie Wilson.Over the course of his career, Jimmy has had the honor to be one of twelve chefs chosen to create and cook a five-course dinner in honor of Julia Child's 80th birthday gala, as well as being one of a select group of Boston chefs to represent the U.S. on a cultural tour and culinary exchange in China. He was awarded Food & Wine's "Honor Roll of American Chefs" in 1983, and in addition to many other news sources, has received critical acclaim in The New York Times, Food & Wine magazine, and The Boston Globe. (*photo courtesy of Jimmy Burke*)

Chef Kevin Conner

As Chief Operating Officer of Community Servings, Kevin oversees all Delivery Department, facilities, and IT needs. The mission of Community Servings is to actively engage the community to provide medically tailored, nutritious, scratch-made meals to chronically and critically ill individuals and their families. Community Servings has evolved from a small neighborhood meals program to a regional program serving nutritionally tailored meals and providing nutrition education to thousands of people per year across Massachusetts — all of whom are unable to shop or cook for themselves or their families due to a critical illness. Chef Conner also oversees Community Servings' Teaching Kitchen program. Kevin, a native of upstate New York, has been a professional chef for 20 years. His culinary experience includes crafting menus and recipes at some of the region's most well-known restaurants, including No. 9 Park, Radius, Union Bar Grille in Boston and Al Forno in Providence. Prior to joining the staff of Community Servings, Kevin worked as the Executive Chef at the Federal Reserve Bank of Boston. Chef Conner is motivated by the significant impact that food can have on someone who is sick and he aims to integrate new recipes and different cuisines into the menu to help ensure that medically tailored meals are flavorful, while still meeting the dietary needs of the clients. Kevin is a graduate of Johnson & Wales Culinary Arts Program. (*photo courtesy of Community Servings*)

Chef Peter Davis

Chef Davis, whose motto is "Fresh and Honest," as in "Fresh from the farm and honest to goodness New England cooking" came to The Charles Hotel with impressive credentials from around the world. After working in high-ranked international hotels including The Hyatt Regency Singapore, The Bali Hyatt, The Grand Hyatt Hong Kong, and The Peninsula Beverly Hills, he returned to his native city of Boston to become Executive Chef at The Charles Hotel in 1995. An avid conservationist with close ties to the fishing and farming communities of New England, Chef Davis was also one of the first proponents of local products. He will not use any genetically engineered foods or products at Henrietta's Table. A true "working chef," heavily involved in the daily operations of the restaurant, the opening of Henrietta's Table was a lifelong ambition. Honored by James Beard Foundation as one of the "Best Hotel Chefs in America," Executive Chef Peter Davis has created a popular, beloved culinary destination and a cult following with Henrietta's Table, located in The Charles Hotel, Harvard Square, Cambridge, MA. (*photo by Susan Seubert*)

Chef Deborah Hughes
and Mary-Catherine Deibel

Mary-Catherine and Deborah met at Peasant Stock Restaurant in Somerville in 1971 and formed a fast friendship there, which transformed into a business partnership with their opening, with Hughes's husband Michael Silver, of UpStairs at the Pudding in 1982—during the exciting period when chef-owned and operated restaurants were just beginning. The emphasis was on season-based, artisanal Italian cooking, inspired at first by Marcella Hazan, whom Silver and Hughes studied with in Italy. Eventually, UpStairs at the Pudding, on the second floor of Harvard's Hasty Pudding Club on Holyoke Street in Harvard Square became a beloved Cambridge eaterie with a broader seasonal menu, catering to Harvard presidents, Pudding Men and Women of the Year, as well as discerning Cambridge diners. Known for its spirit of community and warmth, Mary-Catherine presided over the dining room, talking with every table, while Deborah ran the kitchen and later her famous herb-garden terrace, one of the first and best of outdoor dining rooms. In 2001, Harvard took over the building, and Mary-Catherine and Deborah signed a lease on UpStairs on the Square, an imposing building facing Winthrop Square. There they continued to operate a two-floor dining experience in the Zebra Room and Soiree Dining Room. Given a blank slate, Deborah transformed the restaurant into several different colorful and vibrant environments —it was compared with "being inside a Faberge egg." UpStairs on the Square's reputation for being a hub for the community with a warm and welcoming energy prevailed until its final day—New Year's Eve, 2013. Deborah is happily retired, still cooking and gardening up a storm at her house in Somerville, and Mary-Catherine transferred her front-of-house skills to a life in fundraising, first at Longy School of Music and currently as Director of Development for Cambridge Center for Adult Education. (*photo used by permission of CCTV*)

Chef Todd English

Todd English is a renowned chef/ restaurateur. He is a four-time James Beard Award winner and inductee into the James Beard Foundation's "Who's Who in Food and Beverage in America." Todd has authored six critically acclaimed cookbooks, created the record-breaking housewares line, The Todd English Collection, and hosted the Emmy-nominated and James Beard award winning series Food Trip with Todd English. Todd English Enterprises includes over twenty innovative restaurants spanning the country and abroad, opening the first restaurant, Olives, in 1989. Other concepts include Figs, Todd English Food Hall, Tuscany, Bonfire, Todd English P.U.B, bluezoo, MXDC, and Todd's in Palm Beach. A dedicated philanthropist, Todd is involved with many charities including, City Harvest, Share Our Strength - No Kid Hungry, Big Brother, Make A Wish, among others, and is an honorary board member at Bakes for Breast Cancer. Todd also established The Wendy English Breast Cancer Research Foundation in honor of his sister. (*The photo shows Todd with his sister Wendy; personal photo used by permission of Todd English*).

Chefs Valerie and Ihsan Gurdal

Ihsan was born and raised in Istanbul, Turkey surrounded by a culture famous for its bazaars full of varied flavors and fragrances. Ihsan added his own twist to this mix by becoming a star volleyball player and in 1976 he participated in the Olympics as a member of the Turkish Olympic volleyball team. In 1977, Ihsan left Istanbul to pursue a college education at UC Berkeley. As a student at Berkeley, Ihsan played volleyball and tapped into his natural appreciation of specialty food by working at a local wine shop. In 1982 he took advantage of an offer to become head volleyball coach at Harvard University and left Berkeley for Cambridge, Massachusetts. While in Cambridge, Ihsan kept his interest in food alive by working at a small specialty food store called Formaggio Kitchen. Soon after starting his work at the shop, Ihsan became manager and cheese buyer. Following his retirement from Harvard volleyball, Ihsan was able to put all of his energy into Formaggio Kitchen. In 1992, he took over ownership of the shop and since that time has presided over the shop's development into one of the leading retailers of gourmet foods in the country. He has worked extensively with celebrated cheese makers and affineurs throughout the United States and Europe, including Neal's Yard Dairy of London, Pascal Jacquin of France's Loire Valley, and Paris' Fromagerie Barthelmy. His travels around the world have brought to Formaggio Kitchen an unparalleled selection of rare and unique cheeses and fine foods from around the world. Many have been introduced to the US for the first time and are only available from Formaggio Kitchen. In 2006 Ihsan was inducted into the Guilde du Fromage by Roland Barthelemy and on November 10, 2008 Ihsan received the title of Chevalier of the Ordre du Mérite Agricole from the French government. This title was given to Ihsan for his tireless work in supporting French agricultural artisans by introducing his stateside customers to their hand-crafted products. Other American recipients of this prestigious title include Julia Child, Jacques Pépin, Paul Prudhomme, Alice Waters and Kermit Lynch. Valerie moved to the Boston area from Miami, Florida in 1980 to pursue a college education. Before moving to Boston she spent 6 months living in Madrid with her aunt and uncle. While in Madrid she developed a love for the daily market experience of visiting her local cheesemonger, bakery, meat purveyor and various fruit and vegetable stands. After arriving in Boston she sought out similar shops with an eye for the unique and inspiring and she soon discovered Formaggio Kitchen. While working in the kitchen at the well-respected Cambridge restaurant Chez Nous, she got to know Ihsan from her frequent trips to the shop and in 1984, she decided to work at Formaggio Kitchen full-time. Since then, Ihsan and Valerie have worked together to create in their stores the "market-experience" that inspired their love of food and the desire to share that with their community. (*photos courtesy of Valerie and Ihsan Gurdal*)

Chef Gordon Hamersley

In 1987 Gordon and his wife Fiona opened Hamersley's Bistro in a tiny storefront in Boston's up-and-coming South End. The restaurant's bistro inspired food was unique and simple, inspired by New England ingredients, was an immediate success and Hamersley's Bistro quickly became one of Boston's favorites. Nationally, Hamersley's Bistro received enthusiastic attention in publications like Gourmet, Food & Wine, Fine Cooking and The New York Times. Gordon was awarded the prestigious James Beard Award, has appeared on numerous TV cooking shows and his cookbook, Bistro Cooking at Home, was awarded the IACP award. Hamersley's was closed in 2014 after a run of 27 years. From 2014 through 2016, Gordon wrote a cooking column for the Boston Globe featuring a wide array of recipes. He writes the food column for the magazine, Upland Almanac. Gordon is a respected cooking teacher and mentor to many aspiring young chefs. He teaches cooking classes and students find his ability to relate food history to modern cooking techniques both informative and fun. Gordon and Fiona live in Connecticut. (*photo by Dina Rudick*).

Chef Susanna Harwell-Tolini

Susanna Harwell–Tolini is the Executive Research Chef at Kayem Foods Inc. in Chelsea, Massachusetts. Having studied Culinary Arts at Johnson & Wales University, she has pursued a more technical approach to cooking, and is an active member of the Research Chefs Association. Susanna is not only a Certified Research Chef, but is Chair for the New England RCA Region. Susanna and her husband Edward Tolini ran Le Bocage, a fine dining French Cuisine Restaurant, in Watertown, MA for 10 years. Located near Cambridge, Le Bocage hosted special events for Harvard University, MIT, and several high-tech businesses. Special events included holiday menus; featured menus of cookbook authors Judith Barrett, Marian Morash, and Patricia Wells; and guided wine dinners by Sandy Block, Master of Wine. Le Bocage was rated by the Boston Herald 1996 with 3 ½ Stars and received a rating of "Excellent" from the Zagat Guide in 2000. Chef Edward Tolini has recently retired, but many wonderful memories of Le Bocage live on! (*photo by Katie Smith*).

Chef Michela Larson

Michela Larson was one of the early pioneers in the Boston food renaissance in the 80's and 90's, starting with her ground-breaking Northern Italian restaurant Michela's in East Cambridge. Michela's transition from educator to restaurateur began after living in Europe for 3 ½ years appreciating and learning about Europe's love affair with food and lifestyle. She was determined to bring that love affair to Boston. Michela's mother was born in Northern Italy so the Mediterranean blood was already flowing. Michela's was both innovative as well as a proving ground for many up and coming chefs such as Todd English, Barbara Lynch, Suzanne Goin, and Jody Adams. Her creativity in delivering an exceptional dining experience, along with her eye for talent in the kitchen continued into many other notable restaurants such as Rialto (Jody Adams) at the Charles Hotel, blu (Dante de Magistris) at the Sports Club LA, Rocca (Tom Fosnot, Tiffany Faison), and the blue (Christie Tenaud) at the Boca Raton Resort and Club in Florida. Michela has a 30+ year track record of developing successful restaurant concepts that combine innovative cuisine and sound business operations with a true respect for the past, present and future of a neighborhood. A key ingredient in Michela's success as a restaurant developer and operator is having a passion for community-centric properties that are embraced by the communities in which they live. Unique instinct and talent for creating and nurturing a team culture of energized and engaged staff members adds further to the dining experience. Currently Michela is operating the blue at the Boca Raton Resort & Club after developing the restaurant's new concept and overseeing transition and renovation. Additionally, she works with others who want to develop their own hospitality businesses, such as Farm & Coast Market in Padanaram and Mod Espresso at Modern Relik in the South End. She also serves as co-founder and board member of Community Servings (servings.org), a not-for-profit food and nutrition program providing services throughout Massachusetts to individuals and families living with critical and chronic illnesses.
(*photo by Carol Kaplan*)

Chef Barbara Lynch

As Chef/Owner of the Boston-based Barbara Lynch Collective, Barbara oversees seven celebrated culinary concepts, including No. 9 Park, B&G Oysters, The Butcher Shop, Stir, Drink, Sportello, and Menton. Her cookbook, Stir: Mixing It Up in The Italian Tradition, received the prestigious Gourmand Award for Best Chef Cookbook and she shares her life story through her memoir, *Out of Line: A Life of Playing with Fire*, released April 11, 2017. Barbara is the only female American Grand Chef Relais & Châteaux, and has earned two James Beard Foundation Awards (Best Chef: Northeast and Outstanding Restaurateur) as well as an Amelia Earhart Award for her success in a male-dominated field. In 2017, Barbara was named to the TIME 100, TIME Magazine's annual list of the world's most powerful people. (*photo by Michael Prince*)

Chef Jamie Mammano

From the day that Chef Jamie Mammano opened the doors to Mistral in 1997, his biggest culinary venture yet was destined to become a legend of the Boston dining scene. A graduate of the Culinary Institute of America in New York, Jamie established a reputation for himself amongst the country's most highly regarded chefs. He was the chef for The Jockey Club and Le Pavillion Restaurant in Washington DC, as the chef for the United States Ambassador to Spain, and 10 years spent in the kitchens of the Four Seasons Hotel Company, where he honed his culinary skills at the company's Washington DC, Seattle, Chicago and Boston properties. While serving as Executive Chef for the Four Seasons Hotel Boston, Jamie single-handedly catapulted its dining room, Aujourd'hui, to the #1 ranking in the Zagat Survey of Boston Restaurants in 1995, and soon after readers of Boston Magazine chose Aujourd'hui as the #1 restaurant in Boston and Condé Nast Traveler named it the #4 restaurant in the country. Seeking the next big challenge, Jamie left the Four Seasons, and along with partners Paul Roiff and Seth Greenberg, created the concept for Mistral, a French/Mediterranean bistro in Boston's South End. Through crafting the menu, hiring the staff, handpicking the tableware, choosing the décor and designing the kitchen, Jamie was able to give life to the restaurant he had always dreamed of and that Boston diners could not wait to frequent. Throughout the past 23 years, Jamie and Mistral have consistently delivered excellent food, exceptional service, and garnered numerous accolades including "Top 25 New Restaurants in America" by Esquire Magazine, "Sexiest Bar" by Food & Wine, and four "Best of Boston" awards from Boston Magazine. Jamie has appeared on NBC's "Today Show" as well as CNN's "On the Menu." In June 1999, Nation's Restaurant News named Mistral as one of "5 Hottest Restaurants in Boston" and in July of the same year, Jamie was invited to be a guest chef at the famed James Beard House. Chef Mammano embarked on his second restaurant venture with Mistral partner Paul Roiff in January 2003 with the opening of Teatro, a stylish yet casual Italian-influenced restaurant. With Teatro, Chef Mammano created a comfortable dining spot in Boston's trendy Ladder District, where locals are able to enjoy inspired Italian food and drinks, an open kitchen and playful design. In November 2005, Jamie and Paul followed up their success when Paul made Jamie a partner in The Federalist. The team then opened Sorellina in January 2006, offering regional Italian-Mediterranean cuisine with a modern twist and a unique wine list focusing on hidden Italian gems. In August 2007, The Federalist was transformed to Mooo, a modern steakhouse inside the XV Beacon Hotel. L'Andana in Burlington, MA, opened in October 2007, focusing on Tuscan Wood-Grilled cuisine. In 2013, Mammano and Roiff opened their newest concept, Ostra, a contemporary Mediterranean seafood restaurant. Ostra provides a sophisticated and inviting dining room with an elegant bar and piano lounge, as well as an exclusive private dining space. Their latest venture, Bar Lyon which opened in September of 2018, captures the essence of the bouchon, a traditional Lyonnaise bistro that serves local French cuisine and wine.

(*photo courtesy of Columbus Hospitality Group*).

Chef Frank McClelland

"…food is best when it's in its purest form. My job is to enhance that natural flavor to allow the essence of the food to sing."
-Frank McClelland

Chef Frank McClelland's L'Espalier was a perennial "best" of America's restaurants for three decades, earning top accolades from Zagat, Forbes, Food & Wine, Bon Appétit, Frommer's, Wine Spectator and Condé Nast Traveler as well as nods in international media. L'Espalier was New England's most decorated independent restaurant with seventeen consecutive AAA Five Diamond Awards (the only one in Boston) and eighteen consecutive Forbes (Mobil) Four-Star awards. He speaks and judges across the country at events like Taste of Vail, Foxwoods Food & Wine Festival and the Chefs Collaborative National Summit. The James Beard award-winning chef and cookbook author was early to the farm-to-table or "locavore" dining philosophy, which began while growing up on his grandparents' farm in the White Mountains of New Hampshire. By the age of 25, he had been a chef in two of the most respected Boston kitchens: Harvest in Cambridge and L'Espalier. In 1984, he became Executive Chef at The Country Inn at Princeton in Western Massachusetts where he established himself as a culinary talent who made time to know local farmers. At The Country Inn he earned a four-star rating from The Boston Globe as well as being named one of the country's top 25 new chefs by Food & Wine. Chef McClelland nurtured his love of fresh, regional ingredients and applied his European techniques to create his own signature modern French-influenced cuisine. He then brought his knives back to L'Espalier, purchased the restaurant outright and never looked back. In addition to being the Chef/Owner, Chef McClelland also owned, operated and lived at Apple Street Farm, assuring only the freshest and most local produce, eggs and fowl were available for L'Espalier as well as his rustic French restaurants, Sel de la Terre. His next step has been launching FRANK where he is excited to continue his lifelong commitment to fresh, local, sustainable, season-centric ingredients translated to a more casual, low-key format. He has transitioned his food from 'milestone celebration' to affordable, everyday enjoyment. In order to focus on his direct culinary responsibilities, he sold Apple Street Farm. However, Chef Frank still finds time to nurture a small private farm adjacent to his home in Essex and maintain relationships with numerous local farmers to supply FRANK with the freshest and most local products possible. Chef Frank McClelland is a New England cooking institution, known for developing the Northeast's next generation of exciting culinary talent. His restaurants have nurtured past StarChefs "Rising Stars," and chefs featured in network TV chef shows and industry competitions. Many of Boston's best-known restaurants are populated with alumni who were mentored under his tutelage. (*photo by Ali Strong for OctoCog*)

Chef Moncef Meddeb

Moncef Meddeb was best known by Boston diners as the founder of L'Espalier, died in La Marsa, Tunisia, on March 26, 2019, at the age of 75. He had moved there in 2008. Meddeb's influence on the Boston restaurant scene runs deep; he spent decades in and around the city and opened numerous restaurants. Many local chefs with their own well-regarded restaurants today spent the early part of their careers working for him, and over the course of his own career, he garnered much critical acclaim, including a "Who's Who of Food & Beverage in America" nod from the James Beard Foundation in 1985. "He should be remembered by the new generation of today and decades to come as the most talented pioneer of nouvelle cuisine," said his sister Alia Meddeb, who owns Baraka Cafe in Cambridge and is a chef in her own right. "[He] allowed the old generation to explore new ways and approach how one can express fully his or her potential in marrying cultures and vast flavors when in the mid-'70s in Boston, all special ingredients came from overseas. You can imagine how fortunate anyone felt being part of this journey that took us all to amazing grace land!" Alia also spoke of his "decency, humbleness, and brilliant mind" and noted that he "was funny to the end." Alia Meddeb has graciously allowed us to include Chef Moncef's recipes here to honor his memory. (*photo of Moncef Meddeb on set with Julia Child; Courtesy of Alia Meddeb; photographer unknown*).

Chef Alia Meddeb

Born in Lille, France to a local pastry maker and a Tunisian antiques dealer, Alia Meddeb grew up cooking traditional French and Tunisian dishes in her parents' kitchen, with ingredients sourced from their garden. After attending high school in Tunisia and business school in Massachusetts, she began her career as a line chef at the famous Café Blasé in Provincetown MA and as garde manger at Boston's L'Espalier, where she specialized in pastries, pâtés, and terrines. Her varied career has taken her to the Marquesa Hotel in Key West, Florida and the Hotel Villa d'Este on Lake Como in Italy. She settled in the Boston area in 1993, serving as head pastry chef at Blue Ginger (Wellesley), Ambrosia (Boston), and 8 Holyoke (Harvard Square). She has been head chef at Baraka since 1997. (*photo of Alia and Moncef together; courtesy of Alia Meddeb*).

Chef Marian Morash

"Chef Marian" is best known for work as a television chef on her PBS series, The Victory Garden, which was television's longest running weekly garden series. She is a prolific author; her books include The Victory Garden Cookbook, a James Beard Award nominee, the video/book Victory Garden Recipes, From the Garden to the Table, and The Victory Garden Fish and Vegetable Cookbook, also a James Beard Award Nominee. Morash was a co-founder and executive chef for eleven years of the Straight Wharf Restaurant in Nantucket, which featured seafood and vegetables. She served as executive chef on Julia Child's PBS series, Julia Child and More Company and Dinner at Julia's and also on Child's The Way to Cook home video series, Parade magazine articles, and demonstrations. In 1983, Morash was named to the Food and Wine Magazine "Honor Roll of American Chefs" and received Organic Gardening magazine's "Food Comes First Award." In 1984, she was named by the Cook's Magazine to the first "Who's Who of Cooking in America" of top 50 chefs, an organization which honors the achievements of culinary leaders (now known as The James Beard Who's Who of Food and Beverages in America.) She was the food columnist for the Bostonia Magazine and a food writer for many magazines and newspapers. She has given cooking demonstrations and guest chef appearances around the country. Morash was a founding board member of the Women's Culinary Guild of Boston, and on the Executive Board of the American Institute of Wine and Fook. She is vice president and treasurer of Morash Associates, Inc, a television production company. A BFA graduate of Boston University, Morash lives in a renovated farmhouse with her husband Russell, in close proximity to two married daughters and five exceptional grandchildren. (*photo by Richard Howard*).

Chef Paul O'Connell

Paul O'Connell studied at Johnson and Wales Culinary University. He was the Chef/Owner of Chez Henri, a beloved restaurant in Cambridge, MA for 19 years. Chez Henri carved out a niche for itself by being the only restaurant to serve French food with a Cuban Flair and New England influences. The restaurant was known for Mojitos and the famous Cuban Sandwich. O'Connell uses his cooking skills to raise money for numerous charitable events across the country, and he contributes to programs such as Meals on Wheels and Aid & Comfort. He is an instructor at Le Cordon Bleu College of Culinary Arts, Boston and has also served as a board member of the American Institute of Wine and Food. (*photo by Suzanne Mermelstein*)

Chef Ken Oringer

James Beard Award-winning chef Ken Oringer has built an empire of restaurants inspired by his global travels. Tsukiji Fish Market-style Uni in the Eliot Hotel, Roman enoteca Coppa in Boston's South End, Barcelona tapas bar Toro in Boston and Bangkok, and Little Donkey, serving an entire menu inspired by the chefs' world travels in Cambridge, Mass and Dubai. Ken lives in Boston with his wife Celine, daughter Verveine and son Luca.
(*photo by Elliot Haney*).

Chefs Jacques and Claudine Pépin

Jacques Pépin is a French born, American chef, author, culinary educator, television personality, and artist. He was born in Bourg-en-Bresse, near Lyon, France. After World War II, his parents, Jeannette and Jean-Victor Pépin, owned the restaurant Le Pélican, where Pépin worked as a child. At the age of thirteen, he started his apprenticeship at Le Grand Hôtel de l'Europe in Bourg-en-Bresse. At 16, he went on to work in Paris, training under Lucien Diat at the Plaza Athénée. From 1956 to 1958, during his military service, Pépin was recognized for his culinary training and skill and was ordered to work in the Office of the Treasury, where he met his long-time cooking partner, Jean-Claude Szurdak, and eventually became the personal chef to three French heads of state, including Charles de Gaulle.

In 1959, Pépin went to the United States to work at the restaurant Le Pavillon and studied at Columbia University. He declined an offer from Joseph Kennedy and Jacqueline Kennedy Onassis to serve as chef at the White House. Pépin worked with Howard Johnson's restaurants as the director of research and development for a decade. He has appeared on American television and has written for The New York Times, Food & Wine and other publications. He has authored over 30 cookbooks some of which have become best sellers. Pépin was a longtime friend of the American chef Julia Child, and their 1999 PBS series Julia and Jacques Cooking at Home won a Daytime Emmy Award. He has been honored with 24 James Beard Foundation Awards, five honorary doctoral degrees, the American Public Television's lifetime achievement award, the Emmy Award for Lifetime Achievement in 2019 and the Légion d'honneur, France's highest order of merit in 2004. Since 1989, Pépin has taught in the Culinary Arts Program at Boston University and, served as dean of special programs at the International Culinary Center in New York City. In 2016, with his daughter, Claudine Pépin and his son-in-law, Rollie Wesen, Pépin created the Jacques Pépin Foundation to support culinary education for adults with barriers to employment. (*photos used by permission of the Jacques Pépin Foundation*).

Chef Andrée Robert

After spending 20 years (and a lifetime) at Maison Robert, until it closed in 2004, with her parents, Lucien and Ann Robert, Andrée is a real estate advisor with Engel & Volkers by the Sea on Boston's North Shore. She is enthralled with the warmth of the community and the beauty of the landscape. Helping people fulfill their real estate dreams is a thrill and she is passionate about perfect matches. Preparation and attention to detail are qualities that she honed at the stoves in the Old City Hall in Boston, as executive chef and then general manager, and she continues to strive for perfection. Andrée and her husband Tom Burger were instrumental in the planning, design and building of the Shalin Liu Performance Hall for Rockport Music in Rockport, Mass. Their shared love of music has given them much joy, many uplifting experiences and surrounded them with interesting, positive people. It would be wonderful to put the two lives together and help fellow Bostonians fulfill their real estate dreams on the North Shore! (*photo by Jacquie Gardner*).

Chef Chris Schlesinger

Chris Schlesinger graduated from the Culinary Institute of America (CIA) in 1977. He opened the East Coast Grill in 1986, and then went on to open Jake and Earl's Dixie BBQ and The Blue Room. In 1999 Chris opened the Back Eddy in Westport, MA, overlooking the Westport River. He is the co-author with John Willoughby of five cookbooks: The James Beard Cookbook Award winner, The Thrill of the Grill (Morrow, 1990); Salsas, Sambals, Chutneys, and Chowchows (Morrow, 1993); Big Flavors of the Hot Sun (Morrow, 1994); Lettuce in Your Kitchen (Morrow, 1996); and License to Grill (Morrow, 1997). He has written for The New York Times, and magazines such as GQ, Food & Wine, and Saveur. Chris has taught culinary students at his alma mater, the Culinary Institute of America, in both the New York and Napa Valley campuses. He was the winner of the 1996 James Beard Awards "Best Chef of the Northeast". He has appeared on dozens of television shows around the USA to talk about food and cooking, has been a guest speaker at numerous conferences, and has been featured in over 200 magazine and newspaper articles. Chris is also a founding member of the national organization Chefs 2000 and actively works with local farmers to preserve farming in New England. (*photo by Suzanne Church*).

Chef Michael Schlow

With restaurants spanning the country, Michael Schlow is one of the most influential and respected chef/restaurateurs in America today. His ability to capture a variety of global cuisines and techniques has led to appearances on The Tonight Show with Jimmy Fallon, Bravo's Top Chef Masters, The Today Show, Good Morning America, The Rachel Ray Show, CBS This Morning, Nightline, and The Food Network. Michael has been the recipient of many awards including being named "Best Chef in the Northeast" by the James Beard Foundation, "Best New Chefs In America" by Food and Wine, "Best Chef in the Country" by Sante Magazine, as well as the "Culinary Award of Excellence" given out by Robert Mondavi to just 6 recipients a year. Schlow has spent his life cultivating his craft, learning the restaurant business the old-fashioned way, from the bottom up. Starting as a dishwasher at age 14, Schlow has excelled at every position in the industry. He worked his way up through some of the best restaurants in the world, and now as owner and concept creator, has shown the ability to continually produce restaurants that are critical, as well as financial successes. Esquire, Food & Wine, Conde Nast Traveler, and Gourmet have recognized his restaurants as some of the best in the world. He is the author "It's About Time, Great Recipes for Everyday Life" and is regularly requested to appear and speak about the restaurant and hospitality industry. Originally from Brooklyn NY, Michael travels extensively and enjoys golf, music and photography. He makes his home in Boston, MA with his artist wife Adrienne and his two daughters Petra and Axelle. (*photo by Megan Elstrom*).

Chef Lydia Shire

Lydia Shire attended Le Cordon Bleu in London. She quickly attained national recognition and was given the coveted "Who's Who of Food & Beverage" award by the James Beard Foundation in 1984. She went on to become the first female Executive Chef in the Four Seasons Hotels & Resorts Company to open a luxury property. She has run several prominent restaurants in the Boston area, including Biba, the Excelsior Restaurant, and Pignoli. She was the first female chef of the historic restaurant Locke-Ober, which was ranked the 18th-best restaurant in the country, and was also named as one of the 21 must-visit restaurants in your lifetime. After Locke-Ober closed, she opened Blue Sky at the Atlantic House Hotel in York Beach, Maine and Scampo in Boston's Liberty Hotel – formerly the Charles Street Jail. She has received many prestigious awards including the James Beard Foundation Award as "America's Best Chef – Northeast, Food & Wine's One of America's Top Ten Chefs, the Ivy Award by Restaurants & Institutions magazine, The James Beard Foundation "One of America's Top Five Chefs. She was inducted into the Fine Dining Hall of Fame by Restaurant News. (*photo by Lydia Carmichael Rosenberg*)

Chef Ana Sortun

Ana Sortun is a native of Seattle, Washington and graduated from La Varenne Ecole de Cuisine de Paris in 1989. She opened her first restaurant, Oleana, in 2001 and was named Best Chef in the Northeast by the James Beard Foundation in 2005. That same year she gave birth to her daughter Siena and wrote her first cookbook, *Spice: Flavors of the Eastern Mediterranean*. In 2010, she opened Sofra Bakery and Café with business partner and Pastry Chef, Maura Kilpatrick and several years later they co-authored *Soframiz: Vibrant Middle Eastern Recipes from Sofra Bakery*. In 2013, Sortun partnered with Chef Cassie Piuma to open Sarma in Somerville, modeled after a Turkish meyhane or meze restaurant. Ana is a James Beard Semi-Finalist for Outstanding Chef in 2015, 2016, 2017 and 2019. She is known for bringing Middle Eastern flavors into the mainstream through her passion of Turkish cooking, spices and her husband's (Chris Kurth of Siena Farms) fresh, organic vegetables. Ana is a James Beard 2020 Nominee for Outstanding Chef. Fun Fact—Oleana is Ana's full/real name. Ana is a nickname. Oleana is an old-fashioned Norwegian name that has nothing to do with Turkish food or the Mediterranean but it's also a song and a story about a utopia or promised land!! (*photo by Kristin Teig*).

Chef Ming Tsai

Ming Tsai is the James Beard Award-winning chef/owner of Blue Dragon in Massachusetts and his latest venture BABA at the Yellowstone Club in Big Sky, Montana. An Emmy Award-winner, Ming hosts PBS-TV's Simply Ming, now in its seventeenth season. Ming is the author of five cookbooks: *Blue Ginger: East Meets West Cooking with Ming Tsai, Simply Ming, Ming's Master Recipes, Simply Ming One-Pot Meals* and *Simply Ming In Your Kitchen*. Ming supports many charities including Family Reach, a non-profit whose mission is to provide financial relief and support to families fighting cancer, of which he is currently the President of the National Advisory Board.

For more visit www.ming.com

Chef Richard Vellante

Rich Vellante joined Legal Sea Foods as a chef in our restaurants and became Executive Chef in 1998. He now oversees all culinary operations, developing new recipes and menus as well as managing and training the culinary staff in all our kitchens. A graduate of Hamilton College, he studied at the French Culinary Institute in New York City before spending two years in Italy, cooking his way through several provinces using traditional, farm-fresh ingredients and seafood. He is also the former chef-owner of a three-star restaurant in Massachusetts. Rich was awarded "Executive Chef of the Year" by the Massachusetts Restaurant Association in 2018, earned a Chef 2000 award, was voted "Menu Strategist of the Year" by Restaurant Business and was included among the nation's Top 50 R&D Chefs by Nation's Restaurant News. He has designed numerous dinners for the Confrérie de la Chaîne des Rôtisseurs; he was the first civilian chef in US history to cook for the nation's Senators (2002 and 2004), and he has repeated as guest chef at the prestigious James Beard House and Culinary Foundation in New York City. He also recently attended the executive education program at Harvard Business School. (*photo credit: Legal Sea Foods*)

Chef Jasper White

Jasper White was born in New Jersey in 1954 where he spent much of his childhood on a farm near the Jersey Shore. He credits his love of good food to his Italian grandmother. Jasper began his cooking career in 1973, and after graduating from the Culinary Institute of America, he spent several years working and traveling around the United States. Before settling in Boston in 1979, Jasper worked in New York, Florida, California, Washington state and Montana. In Boston, he teamed up with Lydia Shire –working together at the Copley Plaza Hotel, the Parker House Hotel and the Bostonian Hotel, where they were both propelled into the National spotlight. In 1983, Jasper's Restaurant opened on Boston's historic waterfront. Both Chef and restaurant received numerous awards and were featured extensively in national and local media. In 1990, Jasper was given the James Beard Award for Best Chef, Northeast. After 12 years of being one of Boston's premier restaurant destination, however, Jasper chose to close his restaurant in 1995, and took time to spend with his three young children, as well as write two cookbooks: *Lobster at Home* (Scribner 1998) and *Fifty Chowders* (Scribner 2000). His first book, *Jasper White's Cooking from New England*, was published in 1989. All three books received various awards and critical acclaim. In May 2000, Jasper White surprised people who thought he was inextricably linked to fine dining when he opened Jasper White's Summer Shack, in Cambridge, Massachusetts. Where Jasper's Restaurant had been quietly elegant and formal, Summer Shack is a loud, energetic clam shack. – a Mecca for seafood lovers. The success of the Cambridge restaurant spawned two more Summer Shacks at Mohegan Sun Casino in Connecticut and Boston's Back Bay. From its inception, the Summer Shacks have received enthusiastic reviews from local and national press, including the 2001 James Beard Award Nomination for Best New Restaurant. In 2007 Jasper released *The Summer Shack Cookbook – The Complete Guide to Shore Food*. After more than 45 years in the hospitality and seafood business, Jasper has recently hung up his apron and retired. He now lives most of the year in Cape Cod with his wife, Kathleen, and dog, Buster. (*photo by Bill Aulenbach*)

Chef Michelle White

Chef Michelle White opened Next Step Soul Food Cafe with her mother in 2016. The Codman Square restaurant features Southern cooking classics such as chitterlings, smothered pork chops, fried chicken; collards, macaroni and cheese, candied yams; and sweet potato pie. Chef White credits her love of soul food and cooking first to her Grandmother and Mom who raised and nurtured her in their kitchens. She believes that her food brings people together at the table and being together creates community. Michelle graduated from Community Servings' Teaching Kitchen program. (*photo by Cheryl Richards*).

Chef Douglass Williams

Douglass Williams, Chef/Owner, MIDA Boston, is a Food & Wine Best New Chef 2020, and a James Beard Foundation Semi-Finalist, Best Chef Northeast. Known for his deft technique with hand-made pasta, generous hospitality, and a smile and spirit that light up the room, Williams is committed to making a difference in both the kitchen and the community. Diagnosed with Crohn's disease as a teenager, Williams' path took a left turn, as he learned how to heal himself through food. His journey brought him from his hometown of Atlantic City, NJ to culinary school, and then to traveling the world, learning from the best. From Thailand to Paris, New York City to Boston, he worked and staged at some of the best restaurants, including Radius and Coppa/ Boston, Corton/NYC and Akarme/Paris. While cooking at Coppa, Williams would cycle down Mass Ave where the South End meets Roxbury, and all he saw was opportunity – for change and the chance to create something meaningful. At the corner of Tremont Street and Mass. Ave, he created his first restaurant, MIDA, a neighborhood restaurant inspired by the simplicity of classic Italian culinary traditions. MIDA is one of the city's favorite restaurants, earning top honors for "Best Restaurants in Boston" and "Best Pasta" and is a must-visit when in Boston. Williams shares, "To be a Black chef/owner here in Boston is an honor and a responsibility I take very seriously. I am fortunate to have a successful restaurant, an incredible team and supportive community. I have things to say and share; I try to do it every night through delicious and beautiful dishes at MIDA. And by giving my time and energy to the neighborhood and those around me. I put my passion for story-telling and teaching to use by building bridges in the community through food and conversation. I believe, the world can come together over a delicious bowl of pasta." Williams has two new projects in the works: APIZZA is set to open in the new Hub Hall, Boston and he has just announced plans to open a new restaurant in Newton, MA in Spring 2021. (*photo by Chris Churchill*)

The Mount Auburn Hospital extends its deepest gratitude to the chefs for contributing these recipes.

Julia Child with friends from the Mount Auburn Hospital: Nancy and Kelam Dederian, Debbie and Dr. Larry Mambrino.

Julia's cheerful red apron, auctioned off to support the Hoffman Breast Center, now framed and displayed proudly in the Mambrinos' kitchen.

Acknowledgments

There are so many people to thank, who have supported the Mount Auburn Hospital Hoffman Breast Center over the years in so many ways! It truly takes a village to be successful. It has been my great honor to lead the Breast Center team and collaborate with such wonderful colleagues for a shared passion and purpose.

All of the generous chefs who participated in this project; Jody Adams, Roger Berkowitz, Eric Brennan, Daniele Baliani, Jimmy Burke, Julia Child (with permission of The Julia Child Foundation for Gastronomy and the Culinary Arts), Kevin Conner, Peter Davis, Deborah Hughes, Mary-Catherine Deibel, Todd English, Valerie and Ihsan Gurdal, Gordon Hamersley, Susanna Harwell-Tolini, Edward Tolini, Michela Larson, Amanda Lydon, Barbara Lynch, Jamie Mammano, Andrée Robert, Frank McClelland, Moncef Meddeb, Alia Meddeb, Marian Morash, Paul O'Connell, Ken Oringer, Andrée Robert, Chris Schlesinger, Michael Schlow, Lydia Shire, Ana Sortun, Ming Tsai, Richard Vellante, Jasper White, Michelle White, Douglass, Williams. Special thanks to Mary-Catherine Deibel, Marian Morash, Tim Leahy from Community Servings, and Michela Larson who were instrumental in helping with ideas and guidance. I am grateful for the wonderful cover by Julianne Gilpin, the artwork by Louis Kiley, and assistance with layout and design by Rebecca Maki, transcription by Kayla Pendleton, and research by Nima Olumi.

Alice Hoffman, who had the vision of a world class breast center for Mount Auburn Hospital, and has worked tirelessly to help us make this happen. Joyce Kulhawik, who has been our Emcee Extraordinaire for all Hoffman events. All of the immensely talented authors who have supported the center by reading at our Pink Pages events; Andre Aciman, Diane Ackerman, Christina Baker Kline, David Baldacci, Elizabeth Berg, Judy Blume, Chris Bohjalian, Geraldine Brooks, James Carroll, Christopher Castellani, Susan Cheever, Elizabeth Cox, Anita Diamant, Andre Dubus III, Drew Gilpin Faust, Lisa Genova, Celia Gilbert, Arthur Golden, Doris Kearns Goodwin, Alice Hoffman, Ann Hood, Sebastian Junger, Lily King, Perri Klass, Maxine Kumin, Wally Lamb, Ann Leary, Elinor Lipman, Lois Lowry, Gregory Maguire, Alexandra Marshall, Gail Mazur, Jill McCorkle, Alice McDermott, Mameve Medwed, Claire Messud, Ben Mezrich, Sue Miller, Jacquelyn Mitchard, Celeste Ng, Rosie O'Donnell, Susan Orlean, ZZ Packer, Pamela Painter, Grace Paley, Robert Parker, Tom Perrotta, Jayne Anne Phillips, Jodi Picoult, Marge Piercy, Anna Quindlen, Richard Russo, Anita Shreve, Lauren Slater, Elizabeth Strout, Amy Tan, Jennifer Weiner, Debra Winger, Lee Woodruff.

Our fabulous Pink Pages Committee, Auxiliary members, philanthropic partners, and community advocates; Jill Karp, Gail Roberts, Claudia Scott, Leslie Wolfe, Eileen McDonagh and Bob Davoli, Ellen Canepa, Rosemarie Day, Leslie Arslanian, Karen Biemann, Diane Borger, Christy Cashman, Nancy Freed, Kelly Higgins, Susan Kennedy, Crystal Klaahsen, Anna Whitcomb Knight, Nancy Kolligian,

Alexandra Marshall, Lori Minichiello, Mim Minichiello, Diane Paulus, Janet Prensky, Catherine Shortsleeve, Ellie Harrison Voorhes, Nancy Dederian, Vicky Tomasian, Donna Smerlas. Our partners in Development; Denis Bustin, Katy Keches, Barry Russell, Colin MacLaurin, Michele Urbancic.

Special thanks to Jeanette Clough for her leadership. All of our supportive administration and hospital leaders: John Bridgeman, Greg Herr, Katherine Rafferty, Kelly Hill, Michael O'Connell, Deborah Baker, Rich Guarino, Ed Huang, Yvonne Cheung, Valerie Stone, Peter Clardy, Carey Thomson, Larry Mambrino, Eman Elkadry, Stephanie Page, Mab Butterfield, Jan Ankerson, Susan Donnelly.

So many clinicians who provide such compassionate care to patients and have been champions of the breast center over the years; Lisa Weissmann, Prudence Lam, Carolyn Lamb, Tony Abner, Jean Kim, Terri Silver, Claire Cronin, Melissa Hughes, Mariana Stoleru, Ella Griffiths, John Perry, Linda Covell, Sheida Sharifi, Brinda Kamat, Jacqueline Spencer, Michael Shortsleeve, Pierre Sasson, George Cushing, Leila Khorashadi, Iris Foley, Audrey Frissora, Arpita Swami, Phil Rogoff, Ralph Reichle, Deb Shapiro, Cathy Mintzer, Ginny Palazzo, Sareh Parangi, Jean Fechheimer, Ann D'Avenas, Matt Kaufman, Allison Bailey, Caitlin Connolly, Kelly Kennedy, Laura Boldyrev, Beth Roy, Gabrielle Kovarie, Robin Rahilly, Mary McCullough, Margaret Lotz, Carol McKenna, Janice Saal, Kathy Willey, Denise Natale, Abby D'Angelo, Nicola McNally, Lynn Dreyfus, Kathy Howard, Mary DeCourcey, Nancy Slate. Our caring and capable staff; Sheri Pendleton, Arleen Wall, Sheila Cusack, Kim Mello, Marijean Chagnon, Jennette Paskell, Wei Kwan, Theresa Swartout.

In fond memory of those special physicians no longer with us; Roger Lange, Madeline Crivello, Russell Nauta.

Most of all, family; Chris and Louis, Gabe and Erica, Birdie and Lee, Walter and Mary Ann, Mary Jane, Carolyn, Kathy, Mary Lisa, Michael. And in loving memory of my mother Muriel.

With gratitude,

Susan Pories, MD, FACS

About the Editor

Susan Pories, MD, FACS is the Medical Director of the Hoffman Breast Center, Chief of Breast Surgery, and the President of the Medical Staff (2018-2020), at Mount Auburn Hospital in Cambridge, Massachusetts. Dr. Pories is an Associate Professor of Surgery at Harvard Medical School. She is on the American College of Surgeons (ACS) Board of Governors and is the Chair of the ACS Women in Surgery Committee. She is a Past-President of the Association of Women Surgeons. Dr. Pories is the Associate Co-Director of the Arts and Humanities Initiative at Harvard Medical School and is dedicated to enriching medical education with the arts and humanities. Dr. Pories went to medical school and completed her surgical residency at the University of Vermont.

She completed a Surgical Oncology research fellowship at the New England Deaconess Hospital and a Medical Education Fellowship at Mount Auburn Hospital, Harvard Medical School. Books by Dr. Pories include *The Soul of a Doctor: Harvard Medical Students Face Life and Death*, *The Soul of a Patient: Lessons in Healing for Harvard Medical Students*, *Navigating Your Surgical Career: The AWS Guide to Success*, and *Cancer: Biography of a Disease*.

Dear Friends,

We hope you enjoy these inspired recipes. For safety's sake, please remember to use your best judgment when cooking with raw ingredients such as eggs, chicken, or seafood. Take the time to review all ingredients prior to trying a recipe in order to be fully aware of the presence of substances which might cause an adverse or allergic reaction. Take care when using sharp knives or other cooking implements and be aware of heated cooking surfaces while cooking.

Bon appetit!
Susan Pories and Mary-Catherine Deible

Index